SAINTE-MÈRE-ÉGLISE

© Maurice Renaud, 2014
50480 Sainte-Mère-Eglise
mail : malren@voila.fr
ISBN : 978-2-7466-6834-8

ALEXANDRE RENAUD

SAINTE-MÈRE-ÉGLISE

FIRST AMERICAN BRIDGEHEAD IN FRANCE

June 6, 1944

Translated by Deena Stryker

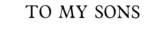

TO MY SONS

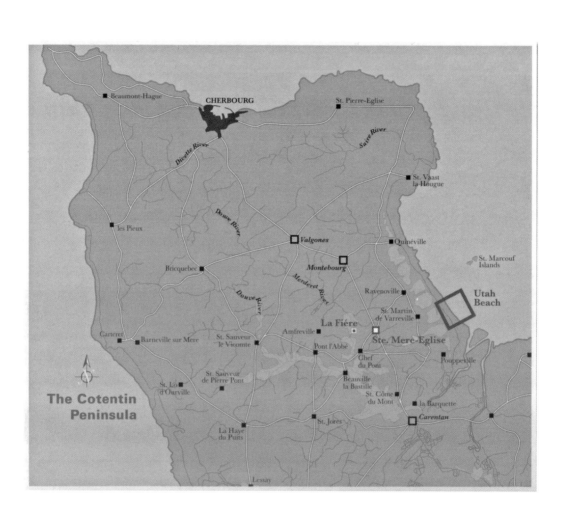

**The Cotentin
Peninsula**

Beaumont-Hague

CHERBOURG

St. Pierre-Eglise

Divette River

Saire River

St. Vaast
la Hougue

Douve River

les Pieux

Valgones

Quinéville

St. Marcouf
Islands

Montebourg

Bricquebec

Merderet River

Ravenoville

Douve River

St. Martin
de Varreville

**Utah
Beach**

La Fiére

Amfreville

Ste. Mere-Eglise

Carteret

Barneville sur Mere

St. Sauveur
le Vicomte

Pont l'Abbé

Chef
du Pont

Pouppeville

St. Sauveur
de Pierre Pont

Beauville
la Bastille

St. Lô
d'Ourville

St. Côme
du Mont

la Barquette

St. Jores

Carentan

La Haye
du Puits

Lessay

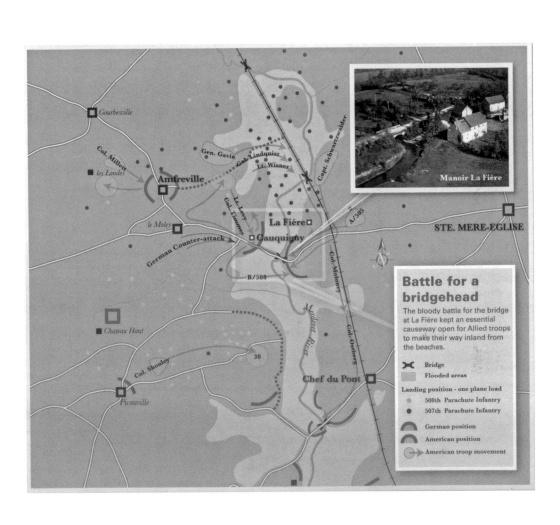

Gourbesville

Col. Millett
les Londes

Gen. Gavin
Col. Lindquist
Lt. Wisner

Capt. Schwartzwalder

Amfreville

le Moley

Lt. Levy
Col. Timmes

German Counter-attack

La Fiére

Gauquigny

N/505

STE. MERE-EGLISE

B/508

Col. Maloney

Chateau Haut

Madael River

Col. Ostberg

Col. Shenley

30

Picauville

Chef du Pont

Manoir La Fiére

Battle for a bridgehead

The bloody battle for the bridge at La Fiére kept an essential causeway open for Allied troops to make their way inland from the beaches.

✕ Bridge
▨ Flooded areas

Landing position - one plane load

• 508th Parachute Infantry
● 507th Parachute Infantry

◗ German position

◖ American position

⟳→ American troop movement

DISTINCTIONS AWARDED TO Mr. ALEXANDRE RENAUD (Lieutenant in WW1) :
WW1 : Medal of Verdun - Medaille Militaire with 3 citations.
Chevalier de la Légion d'Honneur - Chevalier des Palmes Académiques.
Medal of Freedom U.S.A.

LETTER TO SIMONE RENAUD

from
Maurice Schumann

The name of SAINTE-MÈRE-ÉGLISE had already been part of history for several hours when I set foot on French soil near the Asnelles sanatorium at dawn on June 6th, 1944. The vicissitudes of battle delayed by several weeks the moment when I was able to embrace you in a pharmacy that had become famous even in the New World.

But the subject of our first conversation deserves to survive us, as it did our dear Alexander Renaud. As you may remember we had promised one another to tell the world how deserving Normandy had been of the cruel yet marvellous destiny History had dealt her. Devastated, pillaged by air raids, some of which could have been avoided, she could have contented herself with just suffering. Yet, not only by the way she welcomed her liberators, but by the help she offered them, she managed to transform this suffering into sacrifice. As the English, the Canadians, and especially, the Americans — who really needed to be better informed about us — watched, France grew in stature and acquired a better claim to final victory thanks to the Normans. That had been our only goal on June 18th, 1940. This major chapter in the story of our liberation is illustrated by the memories your canton, its mayor, its citizens and you yourself, have engraved in the minds of the young American elite. Never was that truth more evident than the day one of them became the American Ambassador to Paris.

Sainte-Mère-Église

Thus, I owe you a great debt of gratitude, as a fighter on the beaches of Normandy, as a follower of General de Gaulle, but also, and perhaps mostly, as France's Minister of Foreign Affairs. Thanks in great part to you, I was able to speak in the name of a country whose flag flew at the same height as those of the great victors.

George Bernanos wrote : "It may not be very honorable to be French, but it is extremely unwise." Allow me to thank you, my dear Simone, for publishing this basic testimony, which serves to remind our children and our children's children how true this is.

Maurice Schumann
Member of the French Academy

TO THE CHILDREN
OF SAINTE-MÈRE-ÉGLISE

At a "party" organized this summer for the children by the 9th American aviation division stationed at La Londe, I told them they had just lived the most extraordinary fairy tale that anyone had ever dared write for them. During a lovely, moonlit June night, by the light of the fire and accompanied by the sound of the church bells, they saw men with grimed faces, armed with machine guns and daggers, come down from the sky to take the first German outposts. All around them they saw the fighting, the killing, the death of their parents or other loved ones, amidst the noise of the shells and the whistle of tracer bullets. Finally, on June 6th, they saw the huge red, white or green silk parachutes, on the roof-tops, in the trees, fluttering in the sun like immense empty cocoons, finally to end up as shrouds for our dead.

I hope that with the help of this little book, which will tell them exactly what happened, they will be reminded all their lives of this page of history that took place at Sainte-Mère-Église.

Time will have wrought its usual dammage. The real actors will have faded from our minds, other stories will be invented during the coming years by the collective imagination, and the future storeyteller will be able to add tales of fantastic and marvellous acts, without taking anything away from the truth, compared to which our legends, and even the old story of the Trojan horse, will seem quite dull.

À la ville de Ste Mère Église
et ses citoyens courageux
31 le mai de 1956.   M. B. Ridgway

Picture of General RIDGWAY signed :
"To the town of Sainte Mère Eglise and its courageous citizens" dated may 31st 1956.

I

THE PLACE : SAINTE-MÈRE-ÉGLISE

Seen from a plane flying over the Cotentin peninsula, Sainte-Mère-Église probably looks like no more than a tiny strip of houses. It stretches out along Route 13, which starts in Paris, about 20 miles from Cherbourg. To the airplane passenger, nothing would differentiate if from the hundreds of other Normandy villages, shrouded in foliage and flanked by green pastures dotted with apple trees and framed by large elms.

If, on the other hand, you should pass through Sainte-Mère-Église during a trip to Cherbourg by car, you would not be very impressed by the nondescript houses, built without any specific plans over the centuries. But you would admire the large, old, well-proportioned square shaded by chestnut and plane trees. It was here, in the twelfth century, that our ancestors started to build a church, in the prevailing Roman style. In those days, time was unimportant.

People built for the pleasure of building, indifferent to the fact that they might not live to see the finished product. They knew their children and their grandchildren would continue the job. And indeed, it took four centuries before the church was finished, each generation carrying on the task acording to its own taste. Thus, what started out as a Roman monument, ended up as a Gothic one. Finally, like almost all the other churches of Normandy, this one too was topped with a small belfry, called a "clocher à bâtière". There must have been a great celebration at Sainte-Mère-Église that day, but no records of it are left : all the town's archives were destroyed by the revolution, the counter-revolution and the mold of centuries.

About thirty feet from the church there is a Roman military milestone. It stands gracefully erect on granite steps, where it was placed to signal Caesar's legions that an important phase in the pacification of the Gauls had been accomplished. It must have stood at an important crossroads, watching William's ironclad knights march to the beaches whence they would sail for England, with their heavy towers equipped with catapults — the foreruners of our modern-day tanks.

The countryside around Sainte-Mère-Église is incredibly fertile, and the thick grass grows green winter and summer. This is the heart of the Cotentin region, one of France's richest. Generous milk giving cows and thoroughbred riding horses that are the glory of the Vincennes and Longchamp race tracks, pasture in the fields surrounded by thick hedges.

The Germans arrived in Sainte-Mère-Église on June 18, 1940, without firing a shot. The bridges over the swamps of Saint-Côme-du-Mont, between Sainte-Mère-Église and Carentan, had been destroyed, and in the face of heavy gun fire from the French navy, the invaders were forced to retreat toward the roads to Périers and Haye-du-Puits, then circle around the peninsula from the west. Thus, Valognes had been occupied before Sainte-Mère-Église. The telephone lines were not cut, and we were warned in good time by the post offices when the first troops arrived in Valognes and Montebourg.

The Germans immediately occupied the houses, leaving the owners a minimum of space. Then, in the following weeks, formidably armed and well disciplined, they lined up facing the coast of England.

The place : Sainte-Mère-Église

Regiments of tall, strong men, always clean, and polished from tip to toe, marched by proudly, in rhythmed step, singing at the top of their lungs :

Wir fahren gegen England.
(We're marching against England.)

"In three weeks, England will be *kaput*", they would say. Three weeks passed, then several more. Finally, the great attack was announced for mid-September. The troops quartered at Sainte-Mère-Église tried to stifle the almost mystical panic they felt at the idea of taking to sea, by drinking much and eating heavily.

However, the invasion never took place. October arrived, and there was less talk of an attack.

"Glub, glub, glub", teased the children, imitating the sound of a drowning man gasping for breath as the troops passed by. The truth is, these men were fantastic soldiers, but terrible sailors.

At other times, the children would taunt the invadors by walking alongside them imitating the way they marched. Sometimes the guards chased them, but by the end of 1940, the grotesque goose step had been subjected to so much ridicule, that it had been abandonned in combat areas.

The foreign occupation began, with its problems, its sadness, its worries. A huge flag with a swastika was hoisted in the square in front of the town hall. The Ortskommandandtur covered the walls with the first posters in German and French announcing the execution of patriots guilty of sabotage against the occuping army.

Germany rule had begun.

Sunday inspection in front of the church at Sainte-Mère-Église, August, 1940.

Location of the house on fire in the night of june 5/6 th. Today, The AIRBORNE MUSEUM

The German soldiers were very fond of the milk from Normandy cows.

II

WINTER UNDER THE GERMAN OCCUPATION

The winter of 1943-44 had been incredibly quiet at Saint-Mère-Église. Little by little, during the autumn, the German troops had trickled out, leaving only a string of isolated guard posts on the hillside which communicated with one another via telephone and motorcycle runners. The prices continued to rise, and the black market was all-powerful. Both the Germans and the civilians were willing to buy anything, for themselves as well as for the populations in the towns. The only time we were aware of the war was when news arrived from time to time that the allies had bombed the Cherbourg airport or the one near Valognes.

When the sky was clear, sometimes individual planes would circle above, leaving long trails of smoke behind.

"They're coming to mark the terrain", commented a football player. Others thought they were making V's in the air, and that the French pilots were using up gasoline just to come and say hello. The next day the children would come back from the fields loaded with packages of radar jamming strips which were silver on one side and black on the other. At other times, the roads and the fields were littered with German or allied propaganda.

One day we found tracts all along the main road. It was a proclamation signed by the Commander-in-Chief of the Allied army asking us to store up reserves to help sustain the coming invasion. Farmers were instructed to contribute their animals : they would be paid by being liberated. It was a clumsy ploy and no one fell for it.

Every evening, the BBC, broadcasting from London, brought news of Russian victories, and repeated assurances that we would soon be free. "Leave the coastal areas, the strategic areas, industrial areas", we were told. But they had been saying this for so long that no one believed it anymore. In 1943, they had said they were preparing a major offensive. Then Churchill had said : "Before the leaves fall, the Germans will be attacked on new fronts, and there will be intense fighting in the south, the west and the north."

In October, we had sadly watched the chestnut leaves on the church square turn yellow, then gently fall to the ground. Soon it had been the turn of the plane trees to slowly shed their foliage. The winter rains had begun in November, bringing with them the storms that tore away the last leaves and brought waves to the sea. The most optimistic among us would say : "They can't land now. It won't be until spring."

The BBC had stopped predicting when the invasion would take place. They would spend hours explaining that because amphibious operations were so complicated, the Allies needed a long time to prepare.

The Germans scoffed. "The Tommies will never be ready!"

On those cold, wet winter Normandy winter nights, the only things that were flying around were ducks, geese, sandpipers, and sometimes, very high up, plane formations loaded with bombs for German cities, factories or railways depots.

Then, in February, various troop movements took place in the Cotentin peninsula. Sometimes at night we would hear the convoys heading toward the farthermost tip. One night, as we were coming out of the movies, we saw a long convoy of wagons, the horses driven by French peasants under German escort. These peasants came from a long way away and had been requisitioned to drive troops and materiel to the northern part of the department, probably to La Hague. It was the first time we had witnessed this type of massive requisition.

In March, German anti-aircraft troops, dressed in olive drab, the *Flak*, as they were called, arrived at Sainte-Mère-Église. Without asking anyone's permission, they set up camps wherever it suited them. They evicted the teacher and took over the schools. Other than that, they behaved decently.

They were Austrian Tyrolians. Most of them were fairly old, and this small, choice unit that merely had to supply munitions to the troops stationed along the coast was ideal for them. They had no cannons, only trucks, most of which ran on methane, but which stayed parked most of the time under the trees around the square.

At night we would hear them leave, lights dimmed. They would return, then take off again. The *Flak* commander, who was about fifty-eight, and a music critic in civilian life, was more interested in good living than in waging war.

A few days after the anti-aircraft unit arrived, a German battalion came to bivouac in the village. They were awesome : well trained, disciplined, hard on themselves and on us. We hadn't seen a combat unit like that for a long time.

Suddenly, about two weeks later, they left the village and set up camp in the neighboring villages of Gambosville, Fauville and La Coquerie. We heard that route 13 leading from Paris to Cherbourg was now unsafe. Then the requisitionning began. Every day horses and cars were taken for the German mails, for the troops, for pleasure trips, to go to the Carentan station, to bring food to Baupte, for the hospital at Pont-l'Abbé. The Germans took, but they paid. Almost every day and every night troops went out on manœuvers. Sometimes they would cross the town armed to the teeth; their helmuts, the wagons, the horses and cannons were covered with branches. A certain Lt. Zitt, a huge, ungainly fellow, was promoted Commander of the area. He summoned me to Gambosville to tell me in five points what he expected of me, that is, complete obedience to his every wish.

At about the same time, men where being requisitioned every morning. The entire Cotentin region was to be secured by way of a series of land defenses. Under the direction of German non-coms we at Sainte-Mère-Église were supposed to set up the second line. Very few men showed up for work, and the greater part of the labor consisted in eating and drinking. It's true that, with rare exceptions, the German non-coms were not very insistant, and never punished anyone.

Out there, England...

Cutting tree trunks to make obstacles on the beaches...

III

ROMMEL'S CANDLES

On April 17, a colonel in the German engineering corps ordered special teams to be organized for the next day to plant tree trunks. The trees, which had to be over ten feet high, were cut down from nearby and stripped of their branches. Then the teams had to dig holes one meter deep, in staggered rows, twenty yards apart. The trunks were stuck in the holes, then strung together with barbed wire.

"It's in your interest to work quickly", the colonel told us naïvely. "Once the work is done, English planes and gliders wont be able to land, and your country will be safe from invasion. If you don't do this, your cities and towns to be destroyed."

"It's incredible", we commented to each other that evening. "The Germans seem to think the attack will take place in Normandy." Everyone thought this was very funny. Most of us were convinced it could never happen.

Anyway, the work began. The tree trunks looked like giant candles, and during the day the cows had a good time rubbing up against them. The holes were dug very slowly, and very slowly, the trees were cut down, their branches were removed and they were taken to their new sites. The weeks went by, and the work was never finished.

Another thing happened on April 17th : an order was issued by the Vichy government that all the radios were to be brought to the town halls. Normandy was no longer allowed to listen to the BBC, and anyone who did so was threatened with the most terrible punishment.

Two days later, I was called to Gambosville by Zitt. Lounging back in his chair, his feet on a table, he didn't offer me a seat. He wanted all the radios stored in the attic of the town hall right away.

"Those radios belong to their French owners", I answered, "and as long as I am in charge of the town, they will remain where they are."

Furious, Zitt started to yell :

"If the Tommies come, your first failure to execute my orders will get you shot!" and he gestured eloquently.

I told him I understood perfectly well, and that I was used to such threats. They threw me out.

The radios belonging to the inhabitants of Sainte-Mère-Église stayed right where they were, in the attic of the town hall.

As I was on my way home, I realized Zitt also believed the Cotentin peninsula was going to be invaded.

The following week an undeclared war went on between Zitt and me. I never saw him again, but he would send me non-coms and sometimes soldiers. Several times, I refused to comply with his requests because the papers hadn't been signed. The non-coms would come back with Zitt's signature and point to the branch I'd be hung from when the Tommies arrived.

Only one of Zitt's men, a rather gentle, intelligent staff sergeant, was courteous. Sometimes he would take it upon himself to lessen the demands on us. I often wonder what became of him. I never knew his name, only that he was Austrian and that he had travelled a lot before the war.

Suddenly, on May 10th, at 8 a.m., soldiers came and requested ten cars. They also requisitioned all the horses and available men in the occupied villages. At first I thought it was for night manœuvres, and protested energetically in the name of the Hague conventions ; a half hour later I realized what was happening : Zitt and his men were leaving for Vauville.

Rommel's candles

That was quite a weight being lifted from my shoulders, and now I can safely say that if those troups had stayed in Sainte-Mère-Église, the great adventure that took place in early June would have ended very differently for the town and for me.

IV

SIGNS OF AN IMPENDING INVASION

It was almost the end of May. The leaves on the big trees of the church square were a tender green and the chestnut trees were bedecked with their cone-shaped flowers. The sky was turnquoise blue, a color rarely seen in Cotentin, and had been that way for the last two months. The roads and fields were dry. The swamps, which the Germans had flooded, were drying up, notwithstanding the best efforts of the engineers to keep them as high as possible. They gave off a bad smell, especially in the evening, as they had the summer before.

It must have been like that from the Middle Ages up until the time when irrigation began, after the peasants deserted the area because of malaria.

Workers digging trenches at Beuzeville-la-Bastille told me that the fields and bushes were full of mosquitoes. At the Saint-Côme bridge, the swarms were so thick at sunset that you couldn't see the sky.

We wondered what the English were up to.

Were they going to wait for the leaves to fall before they made up their minds?

The air raids were becoming more and more frequent. The bridges at Beuzeville-la-Bastille and at Moitiers-en-Bauptois had been bombed

◀ *Beach defenses.*
Posts topped with mines, and which were underwater at high tide.

several times. Yet these were only two small local bridges that crossed the swamps from east to west. They would only be important if the peninsula were attacked, in terms of preventing German reinforcements from arriving. Some people thought the Allies might pretend to be invading the peninsula in order to catch the Germans off guard, but we were all firmly convinced that if there were an invasion, it would take place in the North, around Dieppe, Boulogne and Dunkerque.

One night, little pamphlets were dropped over the Manor garden. They repeated the orders already given, but also, they described how the American and English paratroopers would be dressed, what the jeeps and light tanks would look like, as well as the bigger Churchill and Sherman tanks. There were even drawings.

"Aw, someone scoffed, those pamphlets are printed in big series, and the fact that they fell here proves nothing. They're probably sending the same ones over the North and as far south as Saint-Nazaire."

I agreed.

Work was now being ordered for the first week in June. The trenches around Sainte-Mère-Église were just about finished. They were not the least bit original, and just wove in and out of the orchards, with the usual shields, just like the ones we dug behind the lines in 1916 and 1917.

The fields of trees or "Rommel's candles" as we called them, were moving along, but slower and slower. The German commander didn't seem very energetic. With the authority he had to punish people, he could have got five times as much work done, and demand that the work be finished by June 1st.

During the entire month of May, German troops were moving up towards Cherbourg. We saw infantrymen and artillery troups camping in our fields, as well as Georgians, and Mongolians with Asiatic features. They were commanded by German officers.

During the second half of May, the artillery set up camp at Gambosville. The officers came to see me at the town hall. They wanted shovels, picks and spades immediately. The place was going to be fortified, and the work had to be finished in five days. I told them there were no shovels or spades left in the village, and that they'd have to search every house to find a few tools. They phoned the Feldcommandantur at Saint-Lô to ask what punishment to met out. He answered evasively. Discouraged, they headed for a hardware store, where, after threatening to take eveything, they managed to get a few tools. Trucks were parked at every exit : on the road to Carantan, on the one to La Fière, outside of Capdelaine, and on the road to Ravenoville.

Mongolians with sinister faces could be seen roaming about the village at night.

Suddenly, three days after they arrived, the cannons were removed and I was asked to supply cars to take food, artillery and munitions to Saint-Côme-du-Mont immediately. Two important generals had come on inspection, and it appeared they didn't like showing off all this materiel.

Once again, Sainte-Mère-Église was left with just the *Flak*.

All the Germans we talked to were convinced there would be a landing in Cotentin.

"You can count your houses, they'll all be knocked out", they would say.

The infantrymen stationed in the area often went through the village on their way to manœuvres.

Only the *flak* remained inactive. The commander sent several men to Mercurey, in Bourgogne, to get some good wine. Life was good to them.

During the night of Sunday, May 29, airplanes were humming in the sky, one squadron after another. Then came bigger planes, their position lights on. They were flying so low we could see them clearly in the star-lit sky.

The instinct which makes people congregate in the face of danger, had brought my entire family together in one room. The children had stopped playing, and now, docile and passive, they huddled near the grown-ups.

We decided not to go to bed, and to pack everything of value in our suitcases.

The planes passed to and fro for an hour, then everything was quiet. Mystified, we went up to the third floor, and looked out the windows from where we had a spectacular view of the horizon. We could see a bright light over the Foucarville/Saint-Martin region. Hundreds of flares were coming down. They disappeared below the line of trees, and it seemed as though a new dawn was rising from the sea. Then other flares appeared and remained suspended in the sky. Amidst the throbbing of the motors, we could hear the whistling of the bombs before they exploded. The windows shook. It was daylight over Sainte-Mère-Église, a violently bue-colored daylight, in which there were no half tones or shadows.

A woman in a nightgown came out to close her shutters. Probably the children were afraid and she felt it was better for them not to hear or see what was going on.

Then planes flew over the road to Ravenoville, just above the new houses, and about twenty parachutes dropped out, drifting toward the west above the town hall, coming down toward the road to La Fière. As they passed by, the machine guns positioned in the belfry shot tracer bullets at them.

What was in the parachutes? Were they men, flares that didn't light up, or food? I never found out. Some Germans whom I questioned the next day told me it was nothing important. One of them showed me a piece of white parachute cloth.

For a long time, as night came again, we waited to see if anything would happen. All we could hear was the sound of airplanes we couldn't see.

All that had happened the night before was that the Eastern Cotentin coast had been bombed.

Aerial view of Sainte-Mère-Église right before June 6th, 1944.

General Eisenhower giving a pep talk to the paratroopers of the 101st division before they took off.

In the cockpit of the « Argonia », a C-47, in England, on May 29th, 1944 : final review of D-Day flight plan by A. Parson (2nd from left) and C. Young (1st to right).

Pilots and paratroopers : last picture before take-off.

C-47s and gliders ready to take off.

In a glider above the Channel... in a few minutes it will land at Sainte-Mère-Église.

Final inspection of equipment.

The loaded down paratroopers board the planes at night.

V

THE PARATROOPERS LAND (NIGHT OF JUNE 5th to 6th)

During the first week of June, the bombardments all around Valognes, on the coast, on the railway line, increased. From the clerk's room in the town hall, we could see the allied planes diving over their targets beyond the belfry at Picauville, then pull up toward the clear, impassive sky. Columns of smoke appeared, blown by the wind. The bombing of the bridges continued.

The mirrors and shop windows shook constantly during the night. In the morning, we would learn that a farm had been hit and its inhabitants torn to pieces. Yet life went on, as before. The bombs seemed to be falling at random, without any definite plan.

"Those clumsy people have missed again", we would say.

All during the night of June 4th to 5th, squadrons of heavy bombers followed one another over the peninsula. There was a high wind, and we wondered what region they were going to bomb. We went to bed very late, worrying all the same. At dawn on June 5th, all was calm.

As usual, the *Flak* were busy with their trucks, and the teams of workers had gone off to plant their "candles".

Around six o'clock in the evening, two little allied fighters emerged from a cloudy sky. They flew very low over the belfry, then circled the village. The Germans shot at them and they disappeared into the clouds. At 8 o'clock, the sky having cleared, we saw them again as they flew overhead in big circles. It was going to be a beautiful night. Before it had even got dark, the noise of heavy planes could be heard again. There were so many of them that it was impossible to tell where they were coming from. Shots were fired from the belfry, the fields and the trenches.

The sky near the coast was lit up again. Again we went up to the third floor, and saw the same sight as the week before, only a little further away, toward Saint-Marcouf: there was that same aurora borealis type of explosions that shook the house as though a giant was ramming it.

We had just stretched out on our beds and were falling asleep when someone started banging on the door. I got up. A man told me a villa was engulfed in flames on the other side of the square at the entrance to Haule Park. The firemen couldn't get the blaze under control. We formed a bucket chain all the way to the pump at the meat market. The men were running with their canvass buckets. They threw the contents into a huge tub. We could see shadowy figures busy among the trees. The wind was bending the flames, and pieces of burning paper and straw were being blown towards the barn, which was twenty meters away and full of straw and wood.

The big bombers passed in great waves from west to east in the sky. The machine guns crossed fire above our heads and hundreds of huge luminous flies whistled, squealed and whispered, sometimes beating against the walls of the burning houses. The *Flak*, in combat fatigues, loaded weapons at their sides, watched us. Bombs falling in the distance shook the earth.

Suddenly the church bell rang dismally several times.

Sainte-Mère-Église was in trouble, and the church was calling for help. Just at that moment, a big transport plane, all lights ablaze, flew right over the tree-tops, followed immediately by others, and yet others. They came from the west in great waves, almost silent, their giant shadows covering the earth.

The paratroopers land

Suddenly, what looked like huge confetti dropped out of their fuselages and fell quickly to earth.

Paratroopers!

The work at the pump stopped, all eyes were raised, and the *Flak* started firing.

All around us, the paratroopers were landing with a heavy thud on the ground. By the light of the fire, we clearly saw a man manipulating the cables of his parachute. Another, less skillful, came down in the middle of the flames. Sparks flew, and the fire burned brighter. The legs of another paratrooper contracted violently as they were hit. His raised arms came down. The giant parachute, billowing in the wind, rolled over the field with the inert body.

A big white sheet hung from an old tree covered with ivy. A man was hanging from the end. Holding onto the branches, he came slowly down, like a snake. Then he tried to unbuckle his belt. The *Flak* were only a few yards away. They saw him. The machine guns fired their sinister patter; the poor man's hands fell, and the body swung loosely to and fro from the cables.

A few hundred yards in front of us, near the sawmill, a big transport plane crashed to the ground, and soon there was a second fire raging.

The belfry sounded the alarm once again.

Now we were directly in the line of fire of the machine gun in the belfry. The bullets hit the ground right near us.

It was a lovely night, lit by large swaths of moonlight.

Meanwhile, a paratrooper appeared suddenly in the midst of the group at the pump. He pointed his machine gun at us, but when he realized we were French, he didn't shoot. A German sentry hiding behind a tree let out a yell and ran away as fast as he could. The paratrooper tried to ask a few questions, but since noone in the group could speak English, he crossed the road and disappeared into the night.

Above the fire, the big planes glided by uninterruptedly, lesting their human cargoes on the other side of the cemetary.

Soon the anti-aircraft gunners, realizing the significance of the event, ordered us to go inside quickly.

We crossed a German soldier on the square.

"Tommy parachutists, all kaput", he said.

And he insisted on showing us the body of a soldier lying hear his parachute.

I couldn't resist going to the garden, from where I had a view of the entire surrounding area. From the house, all I had to do was cross the courtyard on the road to the sea. I crept along the little path beside the stream, which had been widened and deepened at that place for use as a public laundry. Flattened against the slope from the garden above the washing area, I looked at the fairy-like scene. The moon, quite low, lit the water brightly, leaving me in the shadows. The planes continued to fly overhead at top speed, their motors going full blast. The sky was continually lit by stray tracer bullets making zebra-like stripes, and often, the lights seemed to be swallowed up by the enormous fuselages. To the east, the great elms of the Manor were silhoutted like Chinese shadows against the red background of the fire. Uninterruptedly, the confetti continued to fall towards the ground. Huge gliders, attached to the planes by cables, were suddenly cut loose and flew in a huge curcle before landing. The vibrations caused by huge bombs exploding continued to rock the earth.

I tried to imagine the thoughts of the parachutists packed into the planes, then jumping into space, and, I don't kwow why, but my mind took me back about thirty years, to the time when, during a clear night like this, I had left the Bethelainville woods with my regiment to go up to the front at Verdun. The two periods were of course, different, yet they were similar in that they both went beyond humanity. The words I had written in my old diary came back to mind, just as I had set them down so long ago :

The paratroopers land

"One by one, in columns, the companies take to the wooded road that leads to Esnes. Our machine gun column, with its carts, follows the batallion. Heavy artillery fire has just started. The cannon flashes together with those of the explosions make hundreds of lights in the night, which resonates like an enormous copper bassin. We walk in silence ; we feel tiny, diminished, like larvae. Each man is unto himself, holding his life in his hands, weighing it, evaluating his chances of keeping it...

"Tiny hopes, hopes that only project a few hours ahead at a time, sustain us, and each of us holds onto them for dear life, like a drowning man to a lifebelt, without confiding them to his neighbor for fear they might fall apart."

That same feeling of tininess when confronted with that most fearful thing of all : the unknown, and the immensity of the job to be done, must have been beating in the hearts of those men come from so far and tossed in the middle of the night onto a foreign land.

At that moment, a plane appeared above the roofs, to the west of my shelter. To the right and left, the parachutists were fanning out, and two of them landed in the garden. A few seconds later, shadows appeared on the garden wall. A third parachute, the last to come out of the plane, was gliding toward me. Suddenly, I saw the paratrooper start to wiggle on the end of his rope a few yards above my head. Then, with a loud thud, he fell into the river. The parachute, stuck in an apple tree, hung across the path. Weighed down by his supplies, his munitions, tangled up in his cables, the poor fellow was drowning without a cry, without a murmur. Thanks to the parachute, I had no trouble pulling him to the bank. He had lost his helmut, was half unconscious, coughing, spitting, trying to clear the water from his eyes. Then he looked at me, and I saw an expression of surprise on his face.

"Tommy ?" I asked.

He probably didn't understand for he answered :

"Yes."

"Don't be afraid", I said in English.

Then he looked at me again and, I don't know why, felt my hat, then my jacket.

"I am French", I said, laughing, "your friend".

He must have thought he had been taken prisonner, and now, realizing the truth, he quickly freed himself from the ropes.

Like a gentleman, he told me his name :

"My name is..."

Although I tried very hard, I could never remember his name.

"May I help you?"

"Thanks, I must go", he answered, in a calm voice that was in sharp contrast with his thrashing about of a few moments before.

He motioned toward a new wave of planes that had just come over the line of trees standing like powerful sentinels at the end of the pasture, indifferent to the grandiose scene before them.

Following in the wake of the great birds of night, other paratroopers, like the key fruit of elm trees were coming down in silence, and soon the great domes of living silk, silvery in the moonlight, would be one with the grass of the fields.

Of course he must have had orders to join his group, and every minute lost could be fatal to him and his companions. Dripping water, without a gun, he stepped out of his parachute. I took him a little furthe, to the steps leading up to the embankment. He wobbled like a drunkard, but before disappearing, he turned to me :

"The parachute is for you. Good bye." I answered with a little wave. The shadow disappeared, than reappeared at the other end of the garden, went over the wall and was lost forever.

As I crossed the road lit by the last rays of moonlight to return home, I mused that tomorrow, with a different look, under different circumstances, the example and grandure of the "poilus" of 1914 would be repeated here.

In the morning, I came back to get the parachute, which I wanted to keep as a precious relique. Often during the days that followed,

The paratroopers land

I asked the other paratroopers the name of this new Moses saved from the waters, but no one was able to tell me anything about him.

The Germans closed the locks of LA BARQUETTE which flooded the marshes on a very large area. Many paratroopers drowned, unable to swim with the load of their equipment.

Note. A long time afterwards, I received a letter from an inhabitant of Epernay who had put this paratrooper up and told me he had died in the parachute drop over Arnheim.

VI

THE PARACHUTISTS

Gathered in one of the bedrooms, windows closed, at about 2 a.m., we heard a noise of motors on the main highway. The moon had set, so we couldn't see anything. But judging by the shouts we could hear in German, it sounded as though the anti-aircraft unit was leaving. Motorcycles went by as full speed. A few automobiles, their lights out, set off for Carentan. Then all was quiet, except for the sound of the machine guns in the belfry letting off long rounds of fire.

I opened a window slightly : the planes were still flying overhead, but very high up. Once in a while, we would hear a faint, short rattling noise that sounded like a partridge calling its chicks.

Around 3 o'clock, on the square under the trees, the flash of lighted matches appeared, followed by the red glow of lighted cigarettes, then an electric light on the body of a parachutist. By the light of that lamp, it looked as though men were lying at the base of the trees. We whispered about it for a long time : were they Germans or British? Given the situation, we didn't think Germans would be lying on the ground, but standing up or ambushed in houses.

Little by little, the night began to dissolve, and a milky dawn began to filter through. As the contours became more precise, we were astonished to see that the town was occupied neither by the Germans nor the British, but by the Americans. The first thing we recognized were the big round helmuts we had seen illustrated in the German magazines. Some of the soldiers were sleeping or smoking under the trees; others, lined up behind the wall and the town weighing building, stood with arms in hand, watching the Church still held by the enemy. Their wild, neglected look reminded us of Hollywood movie gangsters. Their helmuts were covered with a khaki colored net, their faces were, for the most part, covered with grime, like those of mystery book heroes.

Since we were used to the stiffness and impeccable appearance of the Germans, the Americans' uniforms really seemed neglected to us. Instead of boots, they wore brown shoes topped with leather gaiters. Machine gun cartridge belts were slung over their shoulders, then draped around their waists. In addition to their machine guns, each man had a huge revolver strapped to his thigh. They cut a really inelegant figure in their loose fatigues with gathers, of an indefinable color, somewhere between gray, green and kakhi, and open in front. The tunic had a huge pocket stuffed with amunition and food, and another one for bandages; there were pockets on the pants, too, even along the legs, on the sides and in the back. Besides all this, a dagger in a sheath was strapped to their right leg.

This is how the American soldiers appeared to us for the first time on June 6th, 1944. Once we had a chance to really analyze it, we realized that this outfit, which seemed so ugly to us at first, was just about perfect. It may not have enabled the wearer to strut about like the recruiting sergeants of our bygone kings, but it did enable him to carry a maximum of munitions and food without them getting in his way. It was conceived for war and not for parading.

Meanwhile, a parachutist who looked like all the others came and knocked. I opened the door. He introduced himself:

"Captain Chouvaloff."

He asked my name.

"Would you please tell me where I can find the German commander of your town?"

I offered to accompany him.

"Okay", he said. He offered me some chewing gum and we set off together. He didn't speak. A young man from the town joined us. The captain didn't trust him. He walked with me in front of him, then, taking out his gun, he ordered the youth to kick open the door. The commander, together with his entire anti-aircraft unit, had taken off.

Two weeks later, I was talking about this incident with Captain Chouvaloff, who had become my friend. He excused himself, saying :

"We'd heard so much about the French being collaborators, that we were a bit afraid of you."

Yet, during that night of June 5th to 6th, the French did all that was in their power to help the parachutists. Ladders were set up in the right places along the roofs, and garden doors were left open so they could get through.

When the Germans asked questions, nobody knew anything; when the black-faced soldiers asked, everyone knew, and told, where the Germans were hiding. Paratroopers who had strayed as far as Saint-Germain-de-Tournebut and Quineville, were brought back to their units by Frenchmen who led them through the night over more than ten kilometers.

Two Frenchmen, a father and son, led American paratroopers through the marshes of Appeville, with the hills above occupied by the Germans. They had decided to help them reach their units near Saint-Côme-du-Mont. Wading in water that sometimes came up to their knees, they hurried along, often in the open. A German patrol saw them and started furiously blasting the water around them. Suddenly, the father fell dead. Notwithstanding his grief and anger, the son continued on his way. He had just lost the person dearest to him, but duty compelled him to go through with what he had undertaken.

The peasants fed many of the paratroopers, who fought alone for five days at Picauville, in the canton of Sainte-Mère-Église. At night, they were invited to the family table, where they quickly drank a bit of milk and ate some black bread before returning to their posts.

The parachutists

Eighty paratroopers were dropped on the other side of the flooded marshes at Moitiers-en-Bauptois. They were completely isolated, and were doomed to be killed or taken prisoner. The well guarded bridges were in the Germans' hands. It was dangerous to cross the swamp by boat during the dark night. Trees stuck up on the surface, there were muddy places, and the year before, in that same area, farmers who had been hunting starlings at night had been drowned.

And yet, the peasants did not hesitate. They took the paratroopers on the flat boats they had kept hidden for several years. Paddling far from the bridges, between the fields of rushes, they took them to the other side, near the village of Montessy. All night, the tiny boats crossed from one side to the other. The peasants could hear the Germans relaying orders as they changed the guard. This help continued notwithstanding the mistrust of the first few days which prevented the paratroopers from making the most of it immediately.

A few days later, Frenchmen were on hand to lead the Americans to their combat stations. The little boats again crossed the black, mysterious waters, which the local inhabitants imagined peopled with gobelins, as though the legendary heroes, Barbey d'Aurevilly and Jean de La Varende were still floating there.

When asked his name and address by an American colonel, a young Frenchman of about twenty answered proudly :

"It's none of your business! I am a Frenchman, therefore I am your friend, and that should suffice!"

Hurry up. We must go !

Many planes crash atop the Normandy hedgerows.

The morning of June 6th, 1944 : the C-47s have just cut lose the gliders loaded with men and munitions and have turned back to England to fetch more.

One of the biggest gliders, a Horsa, bumped into a hedge along the road leading out of Sainte-Mère-Église toward Ravenoville.

Captain Robert Pipper in front of a wrecked glider.

VII

THE MORNING OF JUNE 6th

The sun came up. Many inhabitants had come out their doorsteps and into the square. Everything was quiet; not a bullet, not a shell could be heard. In the trees, on the roof of the church, of the old folks'home, of the town hall, enormous silk parachutes, free of their loads, were floating softly in the air. Other parachutes made great splashes of color on the ground; already, the children were eying them with envy. Everyone was talking about the night's adventures : the paratroopers had come down everywhere : in courtyards, in gardens, on rooftops.

Except in Haule Park, and in an inside courtyard near an by anti-aircraft office on the first floor of a building, the losses had been slight over Sainte-Mère-Église. It really takes a lot of bullets to kill a moving figure in the night.

I decided to go back to Haule Park. A German sentry was lying dead at the entrance. Near the pump, our fire-fighting equipment was pretty much intact. The house, the barn and the stables were still smoldering.

There were dead soldiers hanging from their parachutes stuck in trees. Others, who had managed to get free of their harnasses, were lying on the ground, gunned down anti-aircraft fire while trying to get away. The poor fellow who had fallen into the fire had rolled pretty far from the house as he fought to put the fire out, and his black body was still smoking. A parachute had capped the top of a giant cedar tree, and the man had managed to slide to the bottom.

I went on to a little field : two gliders had landed on a bush. The large wings had been broken, but the bodies of the planes were intact and I assumed the pilots were probably safe. Through the partitions between the cockput and the fuselage, I could see a jeep in one and a truck in the other. A few meters further along, a soldier was lying in a ditch. A neighbor was helping him to drink a big bowl of milk.

Manœuvers were being held in the streets. Units were walking in Indian file, close to the walls, chewing gum, or with cigarettes between their teeth, their weapons under their arms. Reserve units were sleeping without a care in the world in the square and in the Manor garden.

A few bullets were flying on the hills of Capdelaine. Several German prisoners passed by, their hands over their heads. They were being taken to Chef-du-Pont. It was about 11 o'clock when a German shell exploded in the garden ; a few more shells whizzed by and landed a little further on, in Gambosville.

The battle was about to begin.

The assault on the church where Germans were still embushed.

Paratroopers of the 82nd division patrolling the streets of Sainte-Mère-Eglise. Horses and carriages abandonned by the Germans, and a jeep which arrived by glider...

Sainte-Mère-Église, at the intersection of route 13 and the road to the sea.

Main crossroad in Sainte-Mère-Église. US soldiers set up telephone lines.

Main crossroad in Sainte-Mère-Église. Four young wounded women are carried on a US jeep.

Activity is slowly back.

General Marshall Taylor,
commanding the 101st division.

General Eisenhower, Commander-in-Chief of the Allied Forces, with Major General T. Wyche, commanding the 79th division.

Generals Ridgeway and Gavin, commanding the 82nd airborne division.

Lt. Colonel Edward C. Krause, commanding the 3rd battalion of the 505th parachute division. His mission was to take Sainte-Mère-Église.
Picture taken June 9, 1944.

VIII

THE FIRST COMBATS

The fighting forces were as follows : on the American side, one airbone division, the 101st, which had been dropped in scattered formation behind the swamps along the coast, from Ravenonville and Sainte-Mère-Église to Saint-Côme-du-Mont. Its orders were to take the roads leading to the sea, and also, the strong points on the swamps beyond Vierville, Angoville and Saint-Côme-du-Mont.

A second airborne division, the 82nd, under General Ridgeway, had been dropped to flank the 101st on the west. It was to set up a defensive base at Sainte-Mère-Église, by holding route 13 and also set up bridgeheads on the Merderet.

The 3rd battalion of the 505th parachute division under Colonel Ekman, was commanded by Lt Colonel Krause. The second battalion of that same division (under Lt Colonel Vanderworte) had come down in a well-spaced landing to the north of Sainte-Mère-Église, between Haras, Neuville-au-Plain and Beaudienville.

Facing these battalions, was a large German force.

Two companies, as well as the anti-aircraft unit that had escaped from Sainte-Mère-Église the night before were massed to the south, at Fauville.

There were two companies of Georgians under German command to the east, around Beuzeville-au-Plain and the chateau.

To the north and north-west, troops had been arriving from

Fresville, Emondeville and even Montebourg, in Neuville-au-Plain since midnight; they were well armed and had tanks and cannons.

Finally, little groups of men were spread out on the hills above the swamps, at Cauquigny and Amfreville, near the village of La Fière.

Around one o'clock in the afternoon, bullets began to fly above the trees, then the cannons set up in Fauville, in the park of the chateau of Chappey, as well as those on route number 13 at the top of the hill, began to fire tracer shells. They were aiming at the limits of Sainte-Mère-Église towards Carentan. A veteran of the first world war fell. At the same moment, a father, who had been a prisoner of war, was agonizing in his home. Sainte-Mère-Église was paying the price of its liberation.

The shrapnel banged on the roofs like big hailstones. An officer came over and asked us not to take cover in the shelters.

Unfortunately, since the wells were very close to the surface, Sainte-Mère-Église had no deep shelters. Some people who had gardens behind their houses, had dug trenches. But many others, rather than risk being in an unsafe shelter, had preferred the safest part of their house. As for us, we made haste for a ditch near a little fountain, called Saint-Méen, at about a hundred meters from our house, followed by a number of other inhabitants of the town. It wasn't perfect, but it was better than staying under the trees in the square.

As we were leaving, a house caught fire in the main street; a very young and beautiful girl had just been mortally wounded and was dying in her bed; another former first world war prisoner, oblivious to the danger, tried to find out what was going on. He was badly hit, and although he was dying, all he could think about was the safety of his wife.

However, a little while after we had got into the ditch, which we lined with parachutes to protect ourselves from the humidity, other batteries cames into action. It was easy for us to identify them from the direction of fire. These big cannons, camouflaged in the blockhouses near the village of Azeville, were mounted on revolving carriages and could fire in all directions. At the moment, they seemed to be shooting tentatively toward the road to the sea, thirty feet from where we were hiding.

A parachute sergeant named MacLeod, came to chat with us for a few minutes :

"The situation isn't too bad, but the American tanks should already be arriving from the hill. The officers told us the landing hadn't yet taken place because the sea was too rough, and also for other reasons which they didn't explain."

"Don't go out", he added, "there are groups of Germans all over the place. We just got some out of the trench in that big field."

He pointed to a place where I had been two hours earlier with the children to gather up parachutes for our trench. He was still talking to us when shell fire forced him to drop to the ground. When it was over the waved good bye and was off.

1. Highway 13, to the South, towards Carentan.

2. Wreck of a C47 plane shot down with the pilot Lt Cappelluto, the crew and stick n° 66 of 101st airb. div. paratroopers who could no exit. All got killed.

3. Four white spots. Still a mystery.

4. House and barn burnt down during the night of June 5th to 6th.

5. Church square.

6. Weco glider undamaged.

7. Waco glider broken apart when it landed on the power generator.

8. Horsa glider. Pilot Howard Parks.

June 7th - American paratroopers on patrol in front of Mr. Alexandre RENAUD's pharmacy, near the church

During the battle, at the intersection of route 13 and the road to the sea.

Civilians going to take shelter in nearby ditches.

IX

A NIGHT IN THE DITCH

The shadows were beginning to fall on our ditch, and big clouds were gathering in the sky. We had just handed out condensed milk to the younger children. The Americans had set up one of their cannons right near by and the shells were flying over our heads.

Then a German battery of small field guns started to answer back. They hit a clump of trees twenty yards in front of us, near the road to Clarons. Our ditch was caught in the line of fire and we had no protection on that side. The American cannon, which was firing at a considerable distance as far as Turqueville, suddenly shortened its fire and started to tackle the German battery nearby.

In about two minutes, it was wiped out.

Two days later, I went over there to see what had happened. One of the German cannons had been smashed and had rolled into the ditch on the road to Carons, right near the intersection. There were three bodies next to it.

A little before midnight, tragedy struck. A shell exploded right above us; the branches of the trees split and we were covered with dirt, wood debris and leaves. A woman cried out :

A night in the ditch

"I'm hit!"
Immediately, the children started to whine.
"My ear hurts", cried a little one.

A few minutes later, we realized that two meters from where we were, a mother of three, a young, elegant woman, had passed away. There was no visible wound, and her expression was serene : it looked as though she were asleep. Death had caught her as she was distributing the little food she had brought to those around her with her usual generosity.

The night wrapped us in its shadows. Squadrons of airplanes flew overhead, the shells whizzed by screeching overhead, or tore at the trees around us. Machine guns could be heard in the direction of Beuzeville and the village of Beauvais. In the thick shadows, I spied two armed Germans run by our hideout. Then, under the apple trees in the little field, we could make out the figures of men running for their lives, and the others, ready for the kill, galloping after them.

From time to time we could hear the cries of the children calling their mother.

But something in this lugubrious night did soften the horrors of our wake. Our belfry was still intact, and it told us in its sweet voice that we had just obtained fifteen minutes of grace, that another fifteen minutes had gone by.

"Be brave", it said, "it's 3 o'clock..., 4 o'clock..., day is coming..., it's 5 o'clock, the good sun will soon be up to caress the mother and warm the sleeping children."

And we realized that other hearts were beating nearby, sharing our misfortunes.

X

THE BATTLE OF BEUZEVILLE-AU-PLAIN

While we waited for death, gasping in our hole, other dramas were taking place around Sainte-Mère-Église.

At the town line, near the chateau of Beuzeville-au-Plain, the two Georgian companies had been firing all night at the paratroopers coming down in the fields. They had inflicted severe losses. At dawn, realizing it was useless to take the offensive, and that they were surrounded, the Georgians had taken up positions in the chateau and the commons.

All day on Tuesday, attacks and counter-attacks followed each other. The paratroopers had gone to a nearby farm and requisitioned a sixteen year-old boy. They had given him a helmut and a complete American uniform, a machine gun and cartridges. Leading them through the bushes, he showed them the way.

By evening, the Americans had arrived in front of the gate and surrounded the commons.

Victory was near.

Just then, the allied commander realized the munitions were all used up. Guns were only fired sporadically; then the machine guns were abandonned and only rifles were used. Finally, ambushed in the bushes and the ditches, the soldiers waited for the Georgians to come out, their knives ready.

A few exhausted paratroopers took shelter in a farmhouse. They asked the farmer's wife to hide them.

"We have no more munitions", they told her. "The Germans will get us!"

Luckily, since night was falling, and each company feared a trap, neither of them dared go out into the open.

Suddenly, around 10 o'clock, the American soldiers heard the sound of a large squadron coming to their rescue from over the horizon. As they had the day before, the planes passed over Sainte-Mère-Église in long waves, and the great gliders detatched themselves and came to land on the battle fields. The fragile birds landed at random on the black earth : many of them crashed. Eight hundred yards from the chateau, on the alley leading to La Londe farm, with its hundred year old trees on either side, there were at least fifty wrecks pell-mell, with torn bodies all around.

But the sacrifice was not in vain. The machine gun cartridge belts, the grenades and the metal engines were intact.

The battle began again in earnest at dawn on Wednesday.

Inside the chateau, in the big family kitchen, near the great fireplace dating from the Middle Ages, seated on a sofa, the German captain of the Georgian unit was smoking a cigarette. Nearby, his doctor was taking care of the wounded. From time to time a liaison officer came to report on the situation and take orders. The captain listened calmly to the noise of the battle, the bullets hitting the walls, the American grenades exploding in the courtyard and on the hedges around the pond.

It was about noon when a soldier with a flat, Asian face came in. He gave some explanations and handed the captain a paper.

"Take a good look at this man", the captain said to the few civilians gathered in the room. "You won't see him again. He is the bravest of the brave."

And he sent him off with a friendly tap on the shoulder.

Now he stood there, his German officer's cap on his head. He seemed to be thinking hard.

A big fire was burning in the fireplace, lighting up the copper pots. The commons were burning. Cries could be heard, then screams of pain, and the first grimed faces appeared in the courtyard.

The captain poured himself a glass of cider, and before drinking, cried out :

"To your health !"

Then he went toward the door, unarmed, his crop in his hand. He opened the door and, half turning around, said simply :

"Good-bye sirs.".

He disappeared. His body was never found.

The doctor, a major, also got up, and without a word, unarmed and without his cap, went bravely to his fate.

He fell, twenty yards from the door, hit by a bullet.

These were the fanatic, magnificent men the American soldiers had to face here. Neither prisoners nor wounded there were at Beuzeville-au-Plain.

Near the German road sign, soldier Elmer Habbs takes a short rest.

Two paratroopers of the 505th regiment looking at a map.

Main Street, June 6th, 1944. The paratroopers use the various means of transportation left behind by the Germans.

Paratroopers searching houses for remaining Germans.

On the square of Sainte-Mère-Église : a GI washing.

Difficult going in the Normandy orchards.

XI

THE FIGHTING AROUND CAPDELAINE AND LA FIÈRE

There was also heavy fighting at the other end of the village. The Germans had left on Tuesday morning from Neuville-au-Plain, and they were steadily pushing back Lt. Turnbull's paratroopers toward Capdelaine.

They had resolutely taken the offensive at the extreme point of the American advance.

On Tuesday evening, they arrived in the large enclosures a few hundred yards from La Rosière farm, which the inhabitants had luckily evacuated, since it was in flames.

As in the other areas, munitions were lacking until the gliders arrived.

On Wednesday morning, the Germans were in the area of the Trois-Ormes path. Five of their tanks, ambushed at Neuville-au-Plain, backed up the attack and kept firing on Capdelaine.

In the afternoon, they made a supreme effort. Backed up by the five tanks coming from Neuville towards Sainte-Mère-Église, they entered a place called Misery Valley and got as far as Haras. A hundred yards further along was a hill top, and from there the road sloped down into the center of town.

The Americans realized they were in danger. With their admirable courage, disregarding the fact that munitions were running out, they jumped into the fray. They stuck fast to the Germans : camouflaged in deep, narrow little foxholes, they shot at them at point blank range. Then, as soon as the Germans retreated, they jumped out, raising their daggers. Soon Misery Valley was covered with bodies. We found them a few days later : they had fallen into the ditches in long lines, having been stabbed right in front of the field barriers facing the town, by the enemy that had been lying ambush behind the tree trunks the barriers were built on.

According to legend, the name Misery Valley dates from the Hundred Years war, when Sainte-Mère-Église was at this location. Thatched roof houses with cob walls clung to these hillsides in a winding line reaching to the abbey of Noires Terres. One dark winters' day, English troops, including rough, cruel mercenaries common at the time, were retreating toward the sea. They invaded the village, tortured and massacred the inhabitants, hung them, burned them, then, drunk with blood and killing, went and killed the friars in the abbey. The few terrified creatures who had managed to escape came back, all tattered and torn, lived for a few years in miserable huts near the bodies of their loved ones, and finally, died of the pest.

Sainte-Mère-Église was then rebuilt on its present site, on the other slope of the hill, around Courtomer Abbey. The abbey chapel dating from the 12th century was enlarged and embellished, and finally became the parish church.

On June 6, 1944, Misery Valley was once again subjected to war, death and fire. But from now on it will be a Valley of Glory, for it was along its hedges and paths that the German advance toward Sainte-Mère-Église was finally stopped.

All during Tuesday, to the west, near the village of La Fière, which is part of Sainte-Mère-Église canton, the 1st battalion of the 505th regiment, plus various elements of the 607th and 508th, had knocked out the German enclaves set up on the hilltops, prevented the enemy from crossing the bridge, and helped the little detachment that was holding the accesses from Chef-du-Pont to the swamps. As night fell, little foxholes were dug all along the five hundred yard wide swamp.

That night, the situation was tragic. The Germans, advancing from Cauquigny and backed up by three tanks, had slipped along the road and tried to force the heights. Munitions were scarce and the paratroopers had to stop the tanks at point blank range with hand grenades and a bazooka.

The next morning, in full daylight, around 8 o'clock, hedge-hoping rescue squadrons had dropped parachutes with food and munitions. The Germans had fired their cannons, and soon several farms were burning and collapsing.

Meanwhile, the American soldiers grabbed the parachutes with their precious cargo from the current at Cauquigny, sometimes wading in up to their shoulders, getting stuck in the mud and the reeds, under fire from the machine guns on the other side of the water. The bullets splashed the water, the men were killed or drowned in the black waters with their wounds, but the work went on.

At 11 o'clock, the American machine guns, having received some munitions, started firing again. The road and the swamp became a no man's land.

A giant heron, preoccupied by what was going on, took off clumsily; the ducks fled over the surface of the water, distracted by the terrible things men were doing.

Behind the lines, in all the pastures of Saint-Mère-Église, thousands of fine Cotentin cows, the most beautiful bovines in France, were agonizing alongside the men. Their enormous intestines were boiling, and swarms of bees zooned in on the quarry. Other animals, their paws cut by shells, moaned, and the chickens, totally distracted, jumped over the bushes only to be hit a little further along the way.

That evening, reinforcements arrived from the coast. The attack on the swamps began the next day with the capture of the village of Cauquigny, already destroyed by bombs.

A few days later, the inhabitants of the village came back to find the German troops lying alongside the debris, sleeping their final sleep.

Chaplain George WOOD of the 82d A.D. Picture taken on June 9th in front of the foster home where 200 wounded soldiers were assisted.
Chaplain George WOOD came back several times to Sainte Mere Eglise to attend the D Day celebrations.

XII

LAST BATTLES AND THE ARRIVAL OF THE TANKS

On Wednesday, around two p.m., the batteries of Azeville increased their fire in our little area. It was a veritable barrage just above us. From the north, the battle was coming closer. The crackling of machine guns, punctuated by the explosions of hand grenades, reminded us of the noise of flames burning fur trees, only much louder.

It appeared that the Germans were coming back down the slopes of Pointe Colette, and trying to occupy the road to the sea. Il they managed to do this, the American reinforcements would not be able to reach the coast, except by secondary roads. Two paratroopers on their way to the battle jumped into our ditch to rest for a minute.

"We're all out of munitions", they told us. "We didn't find much on the gliders; others had got there before us. If the tanks don't arrive from the coast in a few hours, we're lost!"

"Anyway", one of them added, smiling, "we still have our daggers!"

And with a cheerful "So long!" they disappeared toward the north along the hedges.

Unfortunately, that meant the end was near for us as well. None of us talked about it to his neighbor, but we were all thinking of how the Germans would avenge themselves, of people being lined up against the walls and shot, of the burning and killing that would take place in Sainte-Mère-Église, of the terrible bombing by the American aviation defending its men against the German advance, crushing what would be left of the town and its inhabitants.

The big cannons at Azeville were spitting flames and steel shells. The children were crying, those of the dead woman kept calling their mother, who was still sitting among us. Had the men been alone, they would have stayed there, but with women and children, the situation was unbearable.

We decided to leave and take shelter in a cellar at the entrance to the village. This cellar was not a very safe place, since it was only underground on one side. But at least we would be able to stand up, and be away from the dead woman, and there would be walls to protect us from the flames and the shells. We would hide the children under some straw and blankets, and we would wait to be liberated or killed.

I went to reconnoitre the road. We would have to cross a ditch with a baby carriage, then a field, then a courtyard littered with dead animals.

During a slight lull in the artillery fire, we left our hole like hunted animals in search of a refuge.

The new place was no better than the ditch had been. When we arrived at the cellar, a percussion shell exploded right at the entrance. Stone and iron debris filled the place. Part of our group ran to a dried up watering hole two hundred yards away. One man was killed and another gravely wounded : such was luck, such was fate...

We were prepared for the worst when suddenly, we heard a prolonged roaring over the noise of the shells, the rifles and the bullets. We could hear it distinctly. Nerves taut, we listened...

The roar become clearer, then we also started to hear metallic noises. Suddenly, everything was transformed. Now, in the distance, we could make out a continuous rolling sound. Filled with joy, we shouted :

"The tanks! The road to the sea is freed, the coast is ours!"

And notwithstanding the shells, oblivious to the dangers still surrounding us, we ran to the road.

The American tanks appeared opposite the new houses.

They were small tanks, but for us, they were big and beautiful. We could see the sergeants at the observation posts in the turret, majestic as gods, powerful as giants. They meant victory, and for us, deliverance!

At full speed, they turned at the intersection and started up the hill to the most dangerous point : Capdelaine.

A few seconds later, we heard the noise of their cannons, which would determine the outcome of the battle.

The paratroopers could boast a great victory : Sainte-Mère-Église, the first American bridgehead in France, all of it included in the canton of Sainte-Mère-Église, had been created. The liaison between this area and the coast was now ensured.

This one enclave, cross-crossed by dozens of little roads, most of them twisting and turning, plus the beaches of Foucarville, Audouville, Saint-Martin-de-Varreville, Le Grand-Vey, beaches with hard sand, without rocks, which had suddenly become ports rivalling with the most important ports in the world, were going to enable the immense army and its convoys of matériel and food to flow through France and Europe.

But to take the canton of Sainte-Mère-Église, the paratroopers had killed entire German units, taken 364 prisoners, and lost half their men.

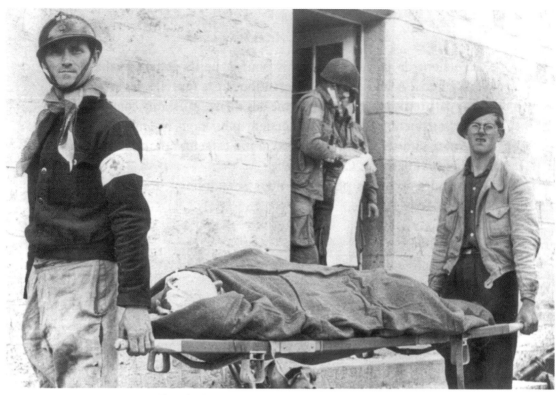

French civilians carry a wounded German soldier.

French civilians and US soldiers carry wounded soldiers away. June 10th 1944.

The first German prisoners in front of the old folks'home at Sainte-Mère-Église. It became the first military hospital, and gave first aid to American, French and German wounded.

A few months later, at the same place, in front of the town hall, a German side-car and a prisoner on the front of a jeep.

◄   *After the fall of Sainte-Mère-Église, two exhausted German prisoners against the wall of a house. The youngest, Ludwig Dresher was nineteen.*

In la Fière, la Couture farm. Wounded US paratroopers and German prisoners.

In la Fière, la Couture farm. German prisoners under surveillance.

In Baudienville US Infantry men coming from Utah Beach take a rest before moving to Sainte-Mère-Église.

US tanks loaded with infantry men going to the front cross German prisoners walking towards the beaches.

Montebourg, June 21, 1944 : the Germans have finally abandonned the poor town to its smoldering ruins.

June 12, 1944 : the American vanguard entering Carentan.

Sainte-Mère-Église : a house on the road to the sea gutted by a shell.

Sainte-Mère-Église : the first jeeps coming up Main Street toward Carentan.

XIII

HOW THE BATTLEFIELD LOOKED

At the end of the day, I couldn't resist going to see the old church and the Roman milestone that had stood on Caesar's invasion route two thousand years ago. The Roman milestone was still intact : yet another war had passed over it without damaging it.

The church too was still standing, but shells had knocked holes in its old walls and one of the butresses had disappeared. Big leprous spots marked the place where bullets had hit the belfry, but the building itself was sturdy and would stand for several more centuries. Calm and serene, unperturbed by its wounds, its voice continued to mark the hour.

The cannons of Azeville had been silence by the tanks. The shell holes in the square were filled with a tangle of branches, beams and the debris of German trucks. A valuable filly and her foal were lying horribly mutiliated near Haule Park.

I passed several men who had bravely volonteered as stretcher and food bearers. They told were coming from Carentan Street and told me that entire families had disappeared, buried under the ruins. A house was still burning, with two bodies inside.

They also told me that several houses had been destroyed in the village of Fauville, whence the first shells had been fired on Sainte-Mère-Église.

Apparently, German corpses were lying all along the ditches in the area of chateau Chappey, pell-mell with the ruined tanks, and the chateau itself was burning. The Americans had set fire to it, thinking it was occupied by the enemy command. The anti-aircraft commander was lying dead in a shelter with the infantry commander. Enemy groups were hiding to the East of Fauville, but they seemed more intent on staying alive than on fighting. The old folks home had been spared, but all the commons had been destroyed.

We had to part. German guns firing from Amfreville had just sighted us. Once again we had to give up the sun and our freedom and go back to the shelter.

The next morning, Captain Chouvaloff came to see me accompanied by another officer :

"Would you please come with me to the police station ?"

I complied. The police had taken shelter in the farm at Beauvais. To get to the village, we had to go up Capdelaine Street then go down the other side and turn into Trois Ormes path.

It was a difficult trip : we ran all the way, keeping close to the walls, under the hail of bullets that rained on the main road.

The battle at the entrance to Trois Ormes and Misery Valley had just ended. Several American tanks were lying in the middle of a field near the Haras, the mouths of their cannons raised toward the sky. On the road at the entrance to the path, two German tanks had been stopped dead in their tracks and been completely gutted. Arms and legs were sticking out of the turrets. The bodies of two unknown soldiers, totally charred, were still smoldering.

Bullets were whistling along the path on which trees had fallen. There were bodies in the ditches.

We hurried : the Germans were only a few hundred yards away.

Photo by Bob Piper, captain of the 82nd parachute division. He was ambushed near the Sainte-Mère-Église old folks'home, waiting for the German counter-attack from Montebourg...

A German tank appears...

... a few seconds later, it is stopped by American bazookas.

FIRST GERMAN PWT
NORMANDY 6 JUNE 1944

German prisoners.

German soldiers killed in a counter attack in Neuville au Plain. To the right the soldier has his eyes open. He tried to throw a grenade to Berge AVADENIAN (505 PIR - 82d A.D.) who shot him few seconds after taking this picture. Quite a unique document !

Two Panther tanks of the Panzer division destroyed by the American 9th division.

German Mark IV tanks destroyed during the counter-attack on Carentan.

US chaplain Francis Sampson blesses dead soldiers. The corps are wrapped in parachutes. In Blosville cemetery (6 000 graves), 2 km South of Sainte-Mère-Église.

Eighteen US chaplains together with the priest of Sainte-Mère-Église (in the center) praying over US graves. Cemetery n° 1.

A US priest celebrates a mass in the cemetery. US soldiers and French civilians attend, honoring soldiers who died to liberate our village.

Lower part : cemetery n° 1 (3 000 graves). Upper part : cemetery n° 2 (5 000 graves).

XIV

THE DEAD AND THE HOMELESS

On Friday afternoon, we buried our dead. There was no official delegation : we were alone with them.

Only a small part of the canton of Sainte-Mère-Église, out of the whole Cotentin, had been liberated. The rest was still been fought over. Many men had come to dig trenches. Others went to and fro with wheelbarrows, fetching the bodies that had been trapped in the ruins.

Since there were no burial shrouds, we tore the remaining parachutes from the trees, and our dear ones left for their last journey wrapped in these great sails of pure silk.

They couldn't be brought into the church, which was serving as shelter for those who had been bombed out of their houses. He who had so loved the underprivileged, had welcomed them by his tabernacle. They slept near Him, rolled in German covers, and from time to time an old woman would come to kneel at the communion table to thank Him for His charity.

However, Christ blessed our dead through the priest, who recited the usual prayers. I lowered the French flag over them and their poor bodies disappeared beneath the earth of Normandy, which recalled them unto her.

Begining on the next day, captain J. K. Owen, then Major Yuill, of Civilian Affairs, ask me for all the available men to go and open other tombs. Alongside the glories of war, was the other aspect, the one with the look of a shadow and the face of a corpse, the one that could just as easily crush the best as the worst.

For days and weeks, our men dug graves in the rich earth, and great white cars with red crosses painted on them, closed like coffins, came in long lines to bring the sacred renmants left after battle.

The invasion troops were now attacking Montebourg, Amfreville, Pont-l'Abbé, and to the south, Carentan.

Pont-l'Abbé was in ruins : smashed and burned by the American aviation.

From the heights of Capdelaine, we could see the fires devouring Montebourg in the distance. Often the German batteries fired on our crossroads. We were like rats who go out after the storm and scurry back to their hole at every threat.

Day and night, without ceasing, without resting, the convoys drove up the hill, bringing men and materiel to the front lines close by. Big tanks crawled up the hill like monstrous scarabs, digging up the top layer of the road cover. Sometimes shells exploded on trucks being driven by black soldiers. Other men would push them into the bushes and the convoy would immediately be on its way again.

A military truck came every morning to let us hear the voice of the BBC. But we already knew everything pertaining to our area.

"They're two days behind!" we would exclaim, laughing.

Several times during the day, officers from headquarters or from the mess, would come down from the nearby lines and tell us :

"We've just taken this or that intersection, this or that field, this or that farm."

And although we had no maps, we knew immediately where the front line was at that moment. Refugees arriving, with their baby carriages, or a little suitcase, or with nothing at all, would confirm the news.

One had no more family, another had left his farm as the flames were engulfing his wife and children; some families had managed to get out of that hell with all their members alive and, to the others, they seemed incredibly lucky.

One evening, the people from the Bon-Sauveur asylum arrive looking like a herd of hunted animals. They were brought by the sisters, and had come by way of Chef-du-Pont road. They gathered around the Roman milestone. Among them were monomaniacs, hysterics, and other mentally disturbed persons; they laughed and made faces, their features contorted. The sisters took them to the church, and recited the rosary to quiet them down. These poor people had instinctively come to hide in the little earthly kingdom of God.

Meanwhile, handfuls of biscuits and chocolate, cigarettes and candy were raining on our childrens'heads, thrown off the trucks by the soldiers on their way to battle.

But on the evening of June 12th, the American Colonel Gann, whom I knew well, and who commanded the Sainte-Mère-Église sector, sent for me as Mayor and asked me to evacuate the population urgently.

"I may need you and a few other men", he added.

He seemed worried, yet I couldn't help but laugh : I thought he was joking. Here at Sainte-Mère-Église were totally euphoric, having just learned that Carentan had been taken. The Americans held Montebourg, nine kilometers to the north, and the 4th infantry division was attacking the big blockhouses of Crisbecq near Quineville. To the west, the Merderet had been crossed, and the 90th US division was striking hard at Pont-l'Abbé. Of course, we were still being shelled, and from time to time some bullets whistled by. But troops and matériel were rolling across the area in great waves from the ocean.

As far as we could tell, the bridgehead was firm. What could possibly happen to us?

But Colonel Gann insisted : "I'm not joking", he said. Finally, after some hesitation, he agreed to tell me what was going on :

« Enemy tanks we didn't even know existed suddenly appeared on the Carentan-Baupte and Carentan-Périers roads. They are waging a furious attack on the 501st and 506th parachute units, who are putting up an extraordinary fight, but nevertheless being pushed back. I've just received an official message from the field command saying that if the tanks manage to retake Carentan, we'll have to evacuate the bridgehead at Utah Beach. All the men we can gather together will be re-embarked and taken to Omaha Beach. That means three or four divisions will have to be taken back to sea. Our warships will ensure a gun barrage to prevent the German troops from advancing. It will be a difficult retreat, and I will ask you to immediately gather as many men as possible to serve as guides for those who may get lost. »

I realized this was a death warrant for most of us, who would be caught between our friends and our enemies!

I promised to do my best. I sent the town crier, to whom I told nothing, to warn the inhabitants of Sainte-Mère-Église and the surrounding area to stay away from route Number 13, and I waited.

Very few of my fellow citizens obeyed. Yet I couldn't divulge the terrible secret, since the news could get out, and also, I didn't want to provoke a panic among the population which had already been sorely tried by the first battles.

The dead and the homeless

At 1 o'clock on June 13th, the colonel told me the first enemy tanks were arriving at the edge of Carentan. American tanks had been requested urgently from the First Army, but they hadn't even landed yet. Air force squadrons had been gathered hastily in England, but it seemed impossible they could get to the battle area in time.

We drank several coffees.

I was worried, and as if to reassure me, Gann smiled and said : « We won't lose the war just because of this little incident. It'll just mean the front will be smaller. »

But that « little incident » meant certain death for so many of my countrymen !

I confess I was afraid until, at dawn, the colonel sent for me. He shook my two hands hard. « The first squadrons have arrived and are hammering at the German tanks. The farthest along are retreating. The Sainte-Mère-Église bridgehead will not fall ! »

Colonel Gann, although he had a military mindset, had certainly not forgotten that in this war, civilian populations were in contact with his troops, and knew how to help them.

XV

A VISIT TO THE LANDING BEACHES

On a beautiful day in mid-June I was finally invited by a Canadian officer, Captain Tanner, of Civil Affairs, an active and cheerful person and an excellent soldier, to accompany him in his jeep to visit the big new landing ports. This was a huge favor, since access to the beaches was strictly off-limits to civilians. But already I was beginning to get the impression that "off-limits" doesn't mean exactly the same thing to Americans as the word "verboten" to Germans.

So we took off via Sainte-Marie-du-Mont, along the back roads bordered with hedges, and which groups of boy scouts were working to widen. Soon, at a turn, we came upon the dunes bordering the ocean.

Hundreds of balloons which looked exactly like monstruous fish were suspended in the sky above us and inland as far as the eye could see. Some were only a few yards above the dunes, others were a little higher, and still others were swaying gently, several hundred meters up. Some of them were lying on the ground, partly deflated. The cables that kept them tied to earth looked like giant algues.

Our jeep, like a poor little spider lost in the midst of these monsters, raced over the tracks covered with thick metal tracks.

Like woodlouse whose dimensions were in keeping with those of the landscape, the ten meter long amphibious "ducks", which had wheels and propellers, climbed up the dunes, deposited their loads, then disappeared once again behind them a fifty kilometers an hour.

June 6, 1944 : protected by naval gun barrages, the landing craft filled with troops rush toward the beach...

First landing of men and matériel on Utah Beach.

June 6, 1944 : the landing craft reaching the beach.

Reinforcements and matériel arriving at Omaha Beach.

Here and there were huge piles of crates that trucks were carrying off toward the roads. All sorts of debris were piled up between the dunes; smashed "ducks", trucks, tanks, boats, metal, as though they had been washed up in some gigantic shipwreck.

Not a single tree remained standing after the great air raids of June; there was nothing but sand and cement blocks torn from the German blockhouses, from which long iron rods were sticking up.

During a long time, it seemed to us, very tiny insects, that we were fliding in the deeps of a vast sea spangled with wrecks, feeled with a huge flora and a prehistoric fauna.

Suddenly, the jeep took a different track and turned off between two dunes. The wheels were no longer squeeking : we were on the beach and the sand was hard.

From Foucarville to Vey's Bay, hundreds of ships had run aground or were still floating. There were little barges, rowboats, tankers, and massive cargoes. All had flat bottoms and stood perfectly upright on the sand. The hull of the cargoes had been opened like closet doors,and from them had emerged jeeps, trucks, tanks and cannons. Cars zig-zagged along the beach between the huge carcasses. At high tide, the latter closed their trap doors and quickly sped off to England.

"Ducks" were constantly arriving from the dunes, coming down to the ocean and entering the water; their propellers beat the waves, and they took up positions alongside the rails of the large floating ships that had remained in the water. Immobile, they allowed themselves to be filled with all sorts of light cargo : men, food, clothing, munitions.

Thus, without wasting time, each cargo would be ready when came the time of day when the tide would allow it to open up and empty its hold.

Heavier equipment and crates were unloaded onto barges that had been sunk end-to-end to form a metal bridge, and trucks and trailers loaded up alongside this new type of wharf.

Above each ship, one of the monstrous fish on the end of a cable kept watch.

In the distance, from the Saint-Marcouf islands to Grandcamp, dark black objects could be see on the horizon. These were the warships garding the entire flotilla.

Before returning to Sainte-Mère-Église, the captain stopped along the coast, near the former village of La Madelaine, in the commune of Sainte-Marie-du-Mont. A few years earlier, this little Normandy village was living a peaceful existence. It included several comfortable properties, half farm, half vacation home. A few hundred meters to the back, in the cemetary where no one had been buried for years, stood a very old chapel. It had a small openwork belfry in which a bell slept as though in a cage. It was surrounded by large trees : yews, oaks and elms, which almost hid it from view. It was an old, unused sanctuary which seemed to have retired there like an old woman behind her windowpanes.

Now, nothing remained of the village, not even ruins. The ground had been turned up, and the few stones that hadn't been pulverized by shells and bombs, had been used first by the Germans, then by the Americans, to pave the roads. The chapel was still standing, but it had been hit in several places and the belfry was awry.

In front of the village, on the dunes overlooking the sea, which were fairly high in this area, the Germans had built a bockhouse. It had been hit by navy shells. We could still see the threatening mouths of the cannons sticking out of the loopholes facing the sea. Inside the enormous mass of reinforced concrete were several compartments separated by armored doors. A metal ladder was embedded into the wall, to enable the lookout to climb to the top from inside and see the horizon with a minimum of danger.

German uniforms were rotting in the lower rooms in sticky, nauseating water, pell-mell with biscuits, cans of food, bandages, equip-

American shock troops arriving on the beach, June 6, 1944.

Doctors of the 4th infantry division attending to the first wounded at Utah Beach.

Utah Beach, June, 6, 1944 : troops from the 4th division of the 82nd infantry regiment resting for a moment along the dike in front of the sea, while the engineers blow up the mines, clearing the way along the dunes.

June 8th 1944. Utah Beach. Reinforcements are coming in.

Saint-Martin-de-Varreville. On the ground of a farm just liberated a US officer plans a new mission.

ment, grenades and pieces of weapons. It was obvious that just a few days ago, a hard battle had been fought here.

Indeed it was right on this part of the coast that the first landing had taken place. It had been followed a few minutes later by a second, a little further south, off the village of Pouppeville.

During that night of June 5th to 6th, the sea had been rough. For long hours, the huge cannons on the warships moored offshore had been firing a barrage of shells all along the coast, hitting the blockhouses, making large breeches in the dike and preventing the German lookouts from seeing the movements of the tansport ships.

Slowly, cautiously, the cargoes loaded with troops, the Landing Craft Infantry, passed in front of the warships and proceeded to within two miles of the coast. Then other small boats took up their positions alongside the cargoes. These were the Landing Craft Vehicles and Personal, which were similar to the "ducks" except that they were not amphibious. Mini gangplanks were thrown from one to the other. The infantrymen, loaded down with their arms, their backpacks, their tools, munitions, tangled up in their life jackets, had to climb into the little dinghies that bobbed up and down on the waves. Between the screams of the shells would come cries for help. Men thrashed about in the deep water, and the sailors quickly fished them out with boat hooks. Some soldiers had strapped their life jackets too far below their armpits because of the load they were carrying, and were drowned, head first, like poorly strung-up fishing floats. As soon as the boat was loaded, it would take off at full speed toward the coast. To save time, it didn't run up on the beach. The captain would guage the depth, and as soon as he knew the men could wade, he gave the signal : "All off!" The order was repeated by the sailors, and at once, all the men jumped into the water. A little line of sharpshooters would form and head for the beach. The boat turned around simultaneously at full speed and was off to get another load.

Around 6 o'clock in the morning, the sun was up, and the first assault wave, completely made up of elite troops from the 4th infantry division, especially selected and trained, reached the edge of the dunes and the dike. They were covered by naval cannons shooting continuously beyond the dunes. However, machine guns from some of the blockhouses were in action. German batteries that had just been set up near the church at Saint-Martin-de-Varreville, were shooting for all they were worth. The shells made enormous geysers in the water or penetrated deeply into the sand.

Other batteries camouflaged ten or twelve kilometers further north, in the woods of Quineville, in the fortifications of Crasville and La Pernelle, were also firing, but they were out of range and were hitting the beaches where there were no boats.

In fact, the American invasion flotilla had adopted a clever strategy : instead of making directly for the disembarkment area, it had headed to the north of the Saint-Marcouf islands, which made the enemy think the landing was going to take place in the large bay between Ravenoville and Saint-Vaast, in the same area where the great battle of La Hougue had taken place centuries before.

Now, the landings continued. When they arrived on the sand, the soldiers dug foxholes, while the vanguard tried to scale the dunes. General Theodore Roosevelt was there, crop in hand, assisted by Colonel Caffee, who was to be in charge of organizing the sector called Utah Beach. As calm as though these were manœuvres, holding a map, the general was giving orders. The first jeep to have landed was waiting for them to climb on board.

At the same time as the first wave of the 4th division, the LCVPs had landed naval observers and the first elements of the 1st special engineering brigade. It was the latter's job to secure pathways for the infantry through the minefields of the dunes at any cost, then to open the dikes to dry out the area that had been flooded by the Germans behind the sea. While the assault waves dug their foxholes, the specialists, followed by infantrymen who protected them, climbed up the dunes and the dike. Using their detectors, they blew up the mines, then marked the path to be followed with long ribbons.

At low tide, the ocean, after washing over them with sand, began to recede from the canoes, the crates and the men. At the edge of the dunes, the line of sharpshooters in ambush was taking heavy losses.

New cargoes arrived, and other waves of men were thrown up on the beach. Little by little, under enemy fire, the 4th division regrouped, ready to attack. A few kilometers inland, the vanguards of the 101st division of paratroopers endeavored to ease the way by dislocating the German formations.

Unfortunately, the cargoes loaded with leavy material, the LCTs, with food, munitions, trucks and tanks, were late. The foamy waves assaulted their hulls. They had had to fight the current and the swell during the Channel crossing.

The infantry waited anxiously.

German planes hedge-hopped over the beach and the sea. They bombed the boats and fired on the foxholes. These aviators were being sacrificed and they knew it; their only concern was to wreck a maximum of dammage before being killed. All of them were shot down by the anti-aircraft guns on board the ships.

Then the American squadrons arrived. They showered munitions and food on the landing area.

It wasn't until the night of Tuesday to Wednesday that the heavy cargoes, the LTCs, reached the coast in significant numbers. They still had to wait for high tide to land. The 1st special engineering brigade went to work. The order was : "Hurry up ! No rest untill the boats have left !" Soaked to the skin, shivering, the men opened the holds, threw the crates from the bridges, gunned the motors, opened the munitions crates, bought out the first amphibious boats. The sick, and the slightly wounded also had to help, until everyone was totally exhausted. By dint of sheer energy, an entire tide was saved !

Sainte-Mère-Église

Aside from three narrow open roads, there was only one usable road through the flooded area : the one called Grand-Chemin, which led to Sainte-Marie-du-Mont and the road to Quettehou. The first groups to venture onto this road were gunned down by the Germans, who were waiting for them, ambushed behind the farm walls. There was no alternative but to wait for the tanks.

The infantry tried to cross the swamps. The enginering brigade had exploded the locks, which in the area are called "tarets", and which the Germans had sealed off with reinforced concrete. The water level dropped. Unfortunately, the swamps turned to mud, and the soldiers got stuck, while the enemy, protected in the woods and behind the bushes on the other side of the water, fired on them.

So, as fast as they could, and by all the roads at once, while the paratroopers got out their daggers and used up their last cartridges, the 70th tank battalion, followed by the 4th, the 90th and the 9th infantry division, overran Sainte-Mère-Église. The lookouts, in full view above the turrets, offered their bare chests to the enemy.

All these magnificent soldiers, fraternally linked to the 82nd and 101st paratrooper divisions, were now going to fight alongside them for many days, sharing their suffering and their glory.

XVI

THE AIR FIELD AT LA LONDE

June 28 th : the Germans continue to resist stubbornly, and yet the front is receding. We can still hear the cannons, but they are far away near Périers and La-Haye-du-Puits. Especially at night, when the wind blows this way, we can distinctly hear the noise of the terrible artillery preparations and the air raids that precede the attacks. The projectors light up the sky, and fighter planes wheel incessantly overhead with a deafening sound, less than a hundred meters above our heads.

A big air field was built only one kilometer from Sainte-Mère-Église, near the La Londe farm. Cranes on trucks, giant power shovels and enormous steamrollers were brought in a few hours, and in less than a week, trees had been cleared away from an area two kilometers long and 800 meters wide and were pulled up like pieces of straw.

The big avenue of trees planted under Napoleon, on which the gliders had crashed on June 6th, had disappeared. There were no more hedges, no more ditches. The terrain had been levelled, covered with long strips running in every direction, and the strips were already covered with tracks as on the coastal roads.

"It looks like a piece of Beauce suddenly transported to Normandy", someone remarked. (*Translator's note :* Beauce is the flatest part of France, located in the East.)

There were no hangers, nothing but the farm buildings looking out of place in the middle of the bare terrain, and at the edge of the huge field, khaki colored, pointed tents. The planes shining like silver slept under the sun.

All those wheels scraping the ground had thrown up a huge cloud of dust. The entire landscape was turning gray little by little. Dust reigned over everything; it was now a part of our environment. It coated the bushes — and our lungs, it dried the fields and dirtied the furniture. Sometimes the countryside disappeared in a halo; it looked like a fire had covered the earth and it seemed as though flames might soon shoot up from this opaque smoke.

There was noise everywhere : the sound of enormous motors, of brakes squeaking, and chains clanking, as if there had been a factory nearby. At every crossroads, a military policeman regulated the traffic with majestic, orderly gestures, stopping, or letting by the convoys.

The danger was getting further away. Now mothers could no longer hear the suspicious gurgling of shells sliding across the layers of air; the children were let out, and began to live a fairy tale existence.

First they visited the hundreds of gliders that were sprinkled over the fields around Sainte-Mère-Église. Some of them, intact, looked proud, resting straight on their heavy tires, needing only the help of their powerful brother planes to clim back into the sky. Others were wounded, their wings low but their bodies intact. But most of them were lying in pieces among the bushes and across the paths.

Sometimes, we saw a dark blue wing with a white star in a tree, vibrating in the breeze like the wing of a giant dragonfly.

But they were all shot. It would be too dangerous to risk a plane to bring them back to England. These poor soulless heroes, their bodies made of mere plywood and canvass were useless, and ignored. They were condemned to be burned as soon as the men could get around to it, and after the children had finished playing on their carcasses.

Every day, the little boys climbed up to the pilot seats, grabbed holf of the wheels, while others tried to push the monsters down the hills. Seen from the roads, the children looked like rats, running under the wings, then reappearing on the other side. Little blond or brunette heads stuck up above the cockpits and the fuselages. The bigger ones cut, sawed, scrapped. In the evening, they would come back loaded with their bounty : mica slabs for our broken windows, cigarettes left behind by the pilots, biscuits wet by the dew and now half moldy, bits of silk cable by which the gliders had been tied to the planes, and especially, bits of metal that parents would later throw away, but which, for the little ones, were like jewels.

While the children dissected the gliders, and took everything that seemed of value to them, army camps had sprung up all over the area. Tents sprouted in rows in the fields in a few hours, like mushrooms. Fences were removed, parts of hedges were cut down to let the trucks through. The hay was cut down as though a wave of grasshoppers had come that way, and large paths ran under the apple trees. The cows mooed, trying to get away from these unfamiliar sights. They wandered along the paths, fleeing the omnipresent sound of motors.

Once a kid who was more daring than the others got into one of the camps ; another kid followed ; the soldiers called them and gave them candy. They taught them to say "Okay," "Hello Joe", "Thanks a lot", and other phrases which didn't exist in the dictionary and made everyone laugh. In the evening the kids came back home all excited, and the next day, they brought their friends and the fun began all over.

Soon every camp had its kids, which the soldiers, the nurses, the assistants in caps or police helmuts all spoiled. They were allowed everywhere, even in places off limits. They went to the kitchens where

*US Army Engineers are building a landing strip at la Londe few days after D-Day.
One mile East of Sainte-Mère-Église.*

A B47 on fire after landing at la Londe.

Gas supply. Landing strip at la Londe.

July 1944. Fifty children with A. Renaud Mayor and his wife are guests of US soldiers at la Londe. The little girls wear parachute made hair ribbons.

C'est la guerre ! One does not understand each other but we can still laugh about it.

The front recedes... Alexandre Renaud, the town crier, a Gendarme officer and an American Soldier in early July, 1944.

The population acclaiming the troops on their way to the front.

Laughing over a bottle of cider.

June 7, 1944 : between battles, two paratroopers of the 82nd division are entertained by a French family, the Simons. Alexander Renaud at far left.

they drank coffee and gobbled up slices of pineapple. Soon they became camp ornements and a source of gaiety for the soldiers, like the pidgeons that hang around the towers of Notre-Dame and are treated like special guests by the Parisians. During the movie shows that were given every afternoon, when the star would sing his song :

"I open the trunk,
I open the bag.
And what I saw ?
The picture of my mother-in-law...",

we could hear, over the deep laughter of the men, the high pitched laughter of the children, who certainly didn't understand, but laughed anyway to keep their big friends company.

There were so many different pleasures, that when a ten year old came home at night to hear his mother complain that she'd sent his older brother looking for him, he answered : "I'm so happy I don't care if you spank me !"

A public ward became a camp mascot. He would arrive from his village at dawn and stay until evening. The cooks would give him cans to open. He would slip like a minnow between the jerrycans and the food, and you could see his happy little face even in the tent where the colonel received visitors. Sometimes he would invite his little friends, and together they would go to watch bombs being loaded under the wings of the planes, or motors being fixed. The soldiers would let them climb up into the flying machines, give them a pair of pliers, and let them start to tighten the bolts.

During the month of July, the 9th aviation group (Colonel Young) invited the fifty children of Sainte-Mère-Église to lunch. They arrived in their Sunday best, the girls wearing ribbons in their hair, some wearing beautiful silk dresses made of pieces of parachute. All day they were fêted and treated like distinguished guests. Every soldier had adopted a French child ; for a few hours the child was his. He tried to speak to him in his language, and gave him presents and chocolate.

When the truck left after the party, a spontaneous cry went up :

The air field at La Londe

"Long live America!"
It wasn't an empty shout. The hearts of the children had been won.

One day, we learned that our aviators were going to leave. We went to the camp to see them.
"We move on", they said sadly.
Hidden behind a tent, cuddled up like an abandonned cat, the little mascot was crying, and when they saw him, the soldiers furtively wiped away their tears.
Many times after that, we heard that little phrase : "We move on", and for the children, as for us, it always had the melancholic ring of an adieu.

XVII

THE LECLERC DIVISION ARRIVES

The first days of August were important for Sainte-Mère-Église. Suddenly there were rumors, which were confirmed, that the famous Leclerc division was arriving from Tchad. It had crossed the deserts of Lybia, fighting its way to Tunisia, holding France's honor high.

The veterans of 1914, those who, whithout arms, one against four, had stopped, then pushed back the enemy, trembled with joy.

"The old army isn't dead after all", they mused.

The first elements of the Leclerc division had already landed between Foucarville and Saint-Martin. Many of the inhabitants were gathered along the road to the sea. At sunset, a huge cry went up :

"There they are !"

The tanks appeared near the new houses, and we saw them at the same place and with the same enthusiasm that we had seen the first American tanks two months before. They too meant victory for us !

The crowd threw flowers and applauded. When the column stopped, children climbed up on the turrets and the drivers couldn't get free.

The Americans watched, smiling. American journalists applauded with us, between two pictures. They realized that, for the first time since 1940, on our own land, France, exiled, condemned to death but glorious, resisting and strong, was reunited with the other France, subjugated and wounded.

For a long time, the tanks rolled by. They flew France's colours, the cross of Lorraine, and on the side, under the turret, the names of our regions : Tarentaise, Anjou, Sauternes, Bergerac, Gascogne, Chantereyne, Val-André, Côte-d'Or, Beaujolais, Champagne, Normandie... The macadam road cracked under the weight, and they were shrouded in a big cloud of dust.

The next day, two non-coms from Toulouse and Brest whose truck had broken down came to see us. They stayed a long time with the American officers, tasting the good old wines of France for the first time in four years.

They kept telling us about their confidence and their belief in the future of the country. But what they were proudest of, was that all this modern material they had, had been bought and paid for in cash.

"They wanted to give it to us on credit", they said, "but General de Gaulle and General Leclerc wanted it to belong to us."

The American officers were wide-eyed. They couldn't understand.

Yet both of you, Robin the employee, Boulanger the sergeant, were so true to our French traditions ! The division was your second family. You wanted her to be respected, and for that, she had to be debt free.

"In France", I explained to the American officers, "two of our greatest virtus are thriftiness and love of our homes. When the average Frenchman earns a hundred francs, he divides it in half : the first half he spends, the other he saves to buy himself a field with a little house, a villa or a chateau that will be all his, free of any mortgage and where he will spend his last days in peace."

"The French hate apartment buildings, even if they're luxurious : whether it be rich or poor they like to have their own house ; a house they'll leave to their children, in the hope they'll take good care of it and improve their legacy.

"Even if they say they are internationalists, the French love their country as though it were a big home : they're jealous of it. They rarely decide to leave it, and when they travel the world, if they can they return to die in the country where they were born."

"Also", I told them, "although the French have acquired colonies, that is, fields, which they have paid for in blood, sweat and money, they did their best to govern these territories with love, like their fathers' fields, and they'll never, even in the greatest need, want to sell this patrimony, which is part of their inheritance."

We spoke frankly, as friends. The American officers would say "yes", but I could tell they weren't convinced.

"I had three automobiles", one of them said, "and I bought them on credit."

Another said :

"When I go from one city to another, I always leave my furniture and my house, and I buy another furnished house. That way, I don't have to move."

I couldn't help thinking about our old family heirlooms, all our belongings, each one of which has its history.

We separated after a last toast. Thanks to these two non-coms of the Leclerc army, we had exchanged some ideas, without fear, as men born in countries with different customs, but who share a deep, common love of freedom.

Mme Margueritte Dessoude ,raising her arm .Behind her : Mme Simone Renaud.
Baby held by the soldier : Maurice Renaud.

July 1944 - Enthusiastic welcome in Sainte Mere Eglise to the Free French Armored Division
(General LECLERC)

July 14th 1944. Sainte-Mère-Église.

June 6th, 1945. Mr & Mrs Alexandre Renaud welcoming US paratroopers from the 508 PIR. 82d A.D. visiting back for the first anniversary.

XVIII

AROUND THE FIRE WITH TWO PARATROOPERS
FROM THE 82ND DIVISION

On a damp night in early autumn I had an encounter with two big soldiers. It had been raining all day, and the branches of the bare trees were bending with longs sighs, at times entwining with one another. All around me, drops fell on the sidewalks from the rainspouts. The few people who had braved the weather were hurrying toward their homes nearby. A long pipe was sticking out of the Military Police tent set up under the trees, and thick black smoke was curling out of it. Most of the MPs had fought in the first battles, had been wounded and had been assigned to this easy job during their convalescence. They had been living among us for several months, and we knew them all. Often they would come back from their post at an intersection leading a small child by the hand. They would talk to them like big brothers, would take them into their tents and give them chocolate or candy.

That day, I had come out to close the shutters, when the two men came slowly down the steps on the square and headed toward me. I immediately saw the glorious insignia on their visors : it showed a plane with a parachute opening out from it. Paratroopers! The moment I saw them, the emotions of June 6th came rushing back, especially when I realized they were from the 505th regiment of the 82nd airborne division, the regiment whose name was linked to Sainte-Mère-Église. One had brown hair and was big and strong. The other was also strong, but he was blond and seemed a bit shy.

Both had been dropped over our town during on that famous night. I asked them to come in. Two great eagles had instinctively come back to this little place on our vast earth when they had landed for the first time, before sweeping over Europe.

That night, we had a wonderful party. Both soldiers had been wounded in Holland, and had come to Sainte-Mère-Église to revisit the site of their first exploits, and pray on the tombs of their comrades who had gone to their eternal sleep among us. Before leaving, they visited us, rembering they had spoken to me during those days of fighting.

They stayed with us for a long time, and the whole family busied itself preparing a real Norman dinner, which included several dishes served slowly, slowly partaken of, as in olden times, when life was not a succession of barely glimpsed moving images, but slices of destiny to be enjoyed in a leisurely fashion.

Big logs, former "Rommel candles", plus some trees that had been torn up by shells, burned joyfully in the fireplace. The room, the only one that had been livable since June, and the only one to have window panes, was warm and comfortable. Since there was no electricity, the table was lit by two lamps, one of which had no more glass. The clear steam from the hot soup mingled from time to time with the black smoke of the oil.

After dinner, we lowered the lights as we did every night, to save oil. The table was pushed back and we formed a circle around the fire. I taught the two men, who knew how to kill with a machine gun, a knife, or a grenade, to use a bellows. They had never seen one, and had as much fun making the flames dance as if they had been two children.

I asked them to tell me what had happened to them.

"Okay", one replied, "we're really comfortable here."

"As you know, I belong to the 505th parachute infantry regiment, which is part of the 82nd airborne division. During the first world war, this division distinguished itself in France, somewhere in Argonne, and because of that, it had a great reputation in the United states. That's why, beginning in 1942, it was equiped to serve as a parachute assault division.

"It was made up of men from the 48 states, all of whom were volunteers. They were daring, courageous fellows, never tired, agile and souple, and they were immediately sent to Fort Benning Georgia, for their training.

"They learned their new profession of wild birds. They were taught to fold, and to open, their parachute. They were told that the green striped parachutes were meant to carry men, that the white ones were to be kept in reserve on their chest, or would be used for bazookas, that the gold parachutes were for carrying mortars, the red ones, munitions, the blue ones, machine guns, the green ones, radios and other communications equipment. Then they were turned into acrobates. They had to slide down trees and jump into space, only to be brutally brought up a few feet from the ground. They were taught to row and swim.

"One day, when their bodies were hardened enough, they were sent to fight on the other side of the sea. Their first exploits took place in Africa; then, in July, 1943, near Jela, in Sicily.

"But those were more like rehearsals. We hardly lost any men. The invasion of Sicily, including the landing of paratroopers, only cost us seventeen men in all."

The two men laughed, as if to say ironically : "! They didn't really have to set up such an elite regiment for such piddling business !"

The following winter, in December, 1943, they arrived in England. The high command billeted them in Leicestershire county. I don't know this area, but they told us it was very much like Normandy, with hedges, fields and little villages. The regiment was reorganized and enlarged, then given intensive training for six months. Night and day they were on manœuvres. They learned to dig foxholes in record time, to find their company, to cross streams, to cut through bushes, to choose good hiding places, to set up their cannons, to use German war materials. Sometimes they were taken very far from their camps, and had to get back, day or night, in companies, in sections, in small groups or alone, using a compass.

Twice, during a six month period, they were dropped at night at the entrance to an English village that looked just like Sainte-Mère-Église. The village was inhabited. They took it by assault, and the first time, the civilians, who evidently hadn't been warned, were terrified.

In the spring, they started to hear rumors of a coming invasion and at night, under the tents, they talked endlessly about where it would take place : the great invasion of Europe!

One morning, they were given colored maps without any names. On the maps were swamps, thickets, tiny streams, and winding roads. But everything that could have helped them guess where the place was had been crossed out. A few days later, the maps were taken back, and others were distributed. The countryside looked the same ; there were also swamps and little winding roads. However, it was certain that the invasion plan had been changed in some way. They were told the reason was that the German general commanding the area had moved his headquarters. The paratroopers job being to destroy that headquarters, they had to change the area they were being dropped in to include the new one.

Under the tents, among the camp beds, the betting was high. Most of the men were convinced the attack would take place in Holland, which they knew to be full of swamps. Others thought it would be in Denmark; still others bet on Normandy.

"I was sure it would be Denmark", one of the two said.

"Anyway, we all wanted it to be as soon as possible. We were ready, and we were beginning to find all those months spent in camp pretty long."

I told them we too had found their preparations long. I told them about Zitt and his men, and how they would threaten us.

The first leaves appeared on the trees, and now the coal stoves were no longer being lit in the tents. Spring had come, and like us, on the other side of the Channel, they wondered : "When will the invasion take place ?"

One evening, the commander spoke to them :

"Work, be prepared ; the invasion date is not far off. You can be sure it will take place, but where and when, I don't know any more than you do."

The betting continued. Denmark was now the big favorite.

Suddenly, on the 26th or the 27th of May, came the order to leave. They boarded trucks for an unknown destination. That same day, here, the Mongolian artillery was ordered to take their trucks from Sainte-Mère-Église to Saint-Côme.

"Before nightfall", the paratroopers continued, "we had arrived at an airfield near the coast, at Bournemouth. The civilians had been evacuated inland, and yet the entire camp was surrounded by barbed wire fences. Sentries mounted guard day and night, and it was absolutely forbidden to leave the area, and even, to talk to the fliers. We were very excited : the invasion was about to take place, yet we still didn't know anything. But Denmark was no longer the favorite : it was Normandy. We weren't going on manœuvres anymore. Officers gathered us for lectures two or three times a day.

"Little by little, rumors were spread by the cooks, the officers'mess personnel. We looked eagerly at the big map of France, and although we were not experts in strategy, we couldn't help but put our fingers on the Cotentin peninsula, which stretched out into the water like a great jetty.

"It'll be there", we said.

"On June 3rd, Lt. Colonel Krause ordered a huge blow-up to be posted on the dining room wall. It had been taken a few days earlier from a plane, and was very sharp. He explained to us that we would be dropped in the fields around this village. He didn't tell us the name of the village. A red area with a number on it showed the place where each company would land.

"Our company was supposed to land to the west of the village. We looked at the photograph, wondering in what part of Europe it had been taken...

"Two hours later, we knew this country as though we had lived here. At the entrance to the village, to the west, after a fork, the road ran straight toward a crossing. Then it continued toward the east, while another, larger road, cut into it from north to south. Near that place, there was a big square with trees. Not far from the fork we could clearly see a truck parked on the right side of the road. Men were loading big crates or jerrycans onto it. There were two other trucks parked to the right near the square, and under the trees we could make out other parked vehicles. A nomber of pedestrians were at the main intersection.

"On June 4th, the rumors grew more specific. Well informed soldiers claimed the officers already knew. The latter would give themselves conspiratorial airs, pointing insistantly to the Cotentin peninsula, without a word.

"Then we learned that the attack was postponed. The wind was high, and the ocean was rough. We were very disappointed. But the next morning, the officers told us the plan. The big picture represented Sainte-Mère-Église. Uncensored maps were given out. Every man had four, which he was to study carefully and keep in his pockets. Each company commander also received a small specimen of the picture taken by plane. We were to leave that same evening.

"The day seemed really long. They told us to get as much sleep as we could, and to eat well. They distributed war rations and munitions. Every soldier checked his machine gun and his revolver. We were given final instructions. Around 8 p.m., they brought us some corks. We had to burn some of them with our cigarette lighters, and rub them on our faces and hands in order to be less visible at night when we came down. We were beginning to be quite nervous, but we joked with each other anyway.

"A few minutes later, Lt. Colonel Krause, our battalion

commander, ordered us out onto the field. We were very fond of him, and we had confidence in his courage, as well as in that of his second in commande, Lt. Colonel Vanderwoort.

"In a few minutes", he said, "you'll be leaving for the attack. I'm counting on you, and you can count on me. Tomorrow morning at dawn, if you fight well, the French flag with be floating from the town hall of Sainte-Mère-Église."

I asked the paratroopers why he hadn't mentioned the American flag.

"The Lt. Colonel insisted on the fact that we were landing on allied and friendly territory. It was the French flag that was to fly over France, not the American one." And they added : "But in Italy, it was always our flag that we raised when we had taken a town."

The fire was beginning to die out, and the night was getting cold. We could still hear the drops of rain falling on the ground with a dull noise. I threw a big log on the fire, and our two guests flipped a coin to see who would work the bellows to revive the fire.

Then they continued their story.

"At nine p.m., a little before nightfall, the regiment gathered on the runway. It was an impressive sight. The big C-47s were waiting in long rows. Some of them were testing their motors one last time. We were divided up among the different planes by groups of eighteen, including an officer and a non-com, sometimes two non-coms. One C-47 stood out at the head of the line : it was the commander's. He was going to head the manœuvre. Above the plane there was a sort of dome, lit up like a lighthouse. The pilot told us he was supposed to keep his eye on that light.

It occurred to me that this show of force, which our two soldiers found so impressive, only involved one regiment. To transport this regiment of three battalions, each of four 135 man companies, it took more than one hundred C-47s. At that moment, on other landing fields in southern England, hundreds of other planes were waiting on the runways for other groups of the 82nd and 101st airborne divisions. Some others were hanging the gliders to their silk cables. Yet others had left for the battlefields : they had already flown over us on their way to bombing the blockhouses along the coast.

At 22:45, whistles were blown and the groups of men boarded the planes, on one side. The door on that side had been taken off to alow the men to jump out in case the plane was hit, and also to avoid delays in the manœuvre. The engines were ignited and the planes took off with an incredible roar, carrying the 505th airborne into the night for battle.

"Above the Channel", one of the soldiers continued, "we had no losses. The navy was watching over us from below, and in the sky, when the plane dipped a little, we could see the black shadows of the little fighter planes that were accompanying us. No one spoke. Every man was meditating, reliving his past, thinking of the loved ones he had left in the States, on the other side of the ocean. Through the open door, we could see the moonlight playing on the tops of the waves.

"Suddenly, a red light lit up the inside of the plane. We were arriving over the French coast, to the west of the peninsula, and all the pilots had turned on their light on orders from the commander. This meant : 'Be ready to jump !'

"We stood up. Every man checked his equipment and touched the red handle of the safety parachute. In the purple light, the blackened faces had a strange, demoniac look. The red light went off and a green light came on. That was the order : 'Jump now !' The officer jumped first, then, one by one, the others. The non-com jumped last. I remember two of the men making a quick sign of the cross before jumping."

He continued :

"I was hanging from my parachute in total silence. My ears were humming, my tongue was dry, my throat was tight. Two or three times, I saw some of my friends, quite near me. The earth was coming up fast. I could clearly see the hedges standing out and the puddles, silvery in the moonlight. I could also see the terrifying gunfire and tracer bullets coming toward us in long, luminous furrows. One bullet tore through my parachute, and I heard the silk rip. I tried to make myself as small as possible ; the seconds seemed like hours. Finally it felt like I was in an express train ; the hedges and trees were going by faster and faster. I could clearly hear the crackling of a machine gun. Doing as I had been told, I pulled on the cables to brake the chute. Then I hunched my back, put my head down, and felt the shock of the ground under my feet. I let myself roll on the ground. When I got up, I found myself in a field. I turned on my cricket — a little pocket apparatus every man had been given. Every company had a different way of regrouping ; mine had been told to give two calls. Other crickets answered. I unbuckled my belt : shadows were calling from the hedges close by. I recognized my pal, who's here with me tonight, and others of my group. We had landed exactly where we were supposed to, in a field near the fork in the western road from Sainte-Mère-Église.

"We started walking in the street leading to the crossing, our machine guns ready. We recognized the place where we had seen the German trucks being loaded."

I asked him from what altitude they had been dropped.
Without hesitating, he answered :
"Six hundred feet."

I was astonished. Seeing them from below as they jumped from the planes, we had been convinced they were at 50 or 60 feet.

"It would have been impossible to jump from such a low altitude", they both answered. "We would hardly have had time to open our parachutes, and most of us would have been killed on landing. Our commander has us jump from the lowest possible distance from earth, so that we would be less likely to be shot down, since we couldn't defend ourselves, and that distance was 600 feet."

We had certainly seen a mirage on that summer night.

"You've just said you were defenseless. But I remember having heard, and even read in magazines, that the paratroopers could fire their machine guns while they were coming down."

The two soldiers laughed heartily.

"If anyone wrote that, they've never been dropped by parachute at night in an unknown country. Sometimes you're swinging several meters from one side to the other, and during that time, your body is sometimes facing the sky, sometimes the earth, depending on how the parachute is oriented, and you can hardly see anything. While you're coming down, you're completely isolated, you have a strange feeling of solitude. Once in a while you catch a glimpse of a star, or a hedge, or the moon, or a tree, and those tracer bullets. For anyone to say that in such a situation you could aim and fire on enemy soldiers on the ground is completely ridiculous."

After this parenthesis, they took up their story again :

"We were still walking along the road leading to the intersection, our machine guns ready. We recognized the place where we had seen the pictures of the trucks being loaded. We saw a German in a window shooting at the planes still passing overhead in long waves. The best shooter of our group got him. The German dropped his rifle out the window. We didn't know if he was dead or just terrified.

"The intersection was deserted; the tracer bullets criss-crossed in the sky above us. When we arrived at the crossroads, we saw men with gold caps running, some with buckets of water. We wondered why these men were out on the street. A few of our guys thought they were collaborators and wanted to grab them, or kill them, but the others argued against it, pointing out they were unarmed. No one fired at them."

The poor firemen of Sainte-Mère-Église went home without realizing that their copper helmuts had made them the object of a council of war that night : men hiding in the shadows had decided independently and arbitrarily whether they would live or die.

The paratroopers kept close to the walls, their fingers on the machine guns. They gathered at the place designated for their company on the maps. It was on the Carentan road, which leads from Sainte-Mère-Église toward the south. They immediately dug a few foxholes, then part of the group was sent to patrol the nearby fields and road.

The blond paratrooper said : "It was a little before dawn, just at that time when night begins to dissolve. I was keeping close to the houses on the right side of the street. A few trucks had just passed by. I had fired on them, but they had continued and disappeared towards Fauville. Suddenly, I saw a man come out of a house on the other side of the road. He looked right and left, then cautiously slid along the walls toward the edge of town. He was half dressed and seemed unarmed, but he was wearing big boots and pants that widened out at the thighs, which made me think he must be a German officer. I didn't want to make a mistake, and since he couldn't get away, I yelled our password at him : '*Flash.*' He stopped : '*Was?*' Since I spoke German, I realized that he was an enemy. But I answered : '*Kommen*

sie hier' (come here). He took two steps toward me. At that moment, almost without thinking, I fired my machine gun at him. He raised his arms, his head rolled from right to left, as if trying to catch his balance, and he fell on his back.

"I went into the house; it looked as though it was completely inhabited by Germans. There were no civilians, the offices were in a shambles. Since I was alone, I didn't want to risk going upstairs.

"Day was breaking. The town seemed dead. But I saw a few curtains move discreetly. A girl opened a window. I realized she was signalling to me : 'Don't be afraid. The Germans have gone.'

"My group was set up, and had planted mines on route 13. My pals told me that before daybreak some trucks had arrived on the Carentan road, all lights lit. Since they saw them from afar, they had time to set up the mines and hide in the ditches. The trucks exploded one after the other, then they shot at them and took several prisoners.

"The sun came up. It was quiet. We had the impression we were still in our English village after manœuvres. Little by little, the civilians came out in the street and shook our hands. They told us to be careful, because there were certainly Germans dressed as civilians all around. Also, one of our patrols had found two of our men in the belfry. The Germans had killed them and stripped them of their arms and uniforms. That meant two Germans were somewhere in the area, dressed as American paratroopers. A man came out of a big courtyard, bringing little glasses of amber colored liquor on a tray. We did bottoms up, and it burned our throats so we thought we had been poisoned."

Our two friends were laughing now. That evening, there were also two little glasses filled with the same liquor on a tray. They pointed to it and said :

"It was calvados, the best, exactly like the one you're serving us tonight. We had never drunk this Normandy brandy, but we know it well now, that's for sure. If we stay here any longer, we would love to see that man, whom we didn't even have time to thank."

In the early afternoon, just as the first shells started to fall on Sainte-Mère-Église, our friend the dark haired soldier was at the bedside of one of our townspeople who had been mortally wounded. He had helped to cary him, was bandaging him and giving him an injection.

Then the terrible battle began. The attacks came one after the other. The Germans were leaving Fauville, and were determined to take Sainte-Mère-Église. The Americans shot at them from their foxholes. Their job was made easier by the fact that the big road was a veritable firing range. The enemy bodies were piling up in the ditches along the road.

Then the Germans tried to attack by way of the fields, with the support of tanks accompanied by about a hundred infantrymen. Luckily, the *bazookas* came into action, and the tanks, hit, retreated as best they could. Most of the infantrymen were killed.

"Our wounded were taken to the Sainte-Mère-Église hospital, which had been turned into a first aid station. Our doctor, Captain Lyle Putnam, was very brave. He took care of your wounded as well as our own. Several times we saw him alongside the stretchers, walking with his usual phlegm, indifferent to the bullets bouncing off the walls. Several times, kneeling in the street by a wounded person, he would bandage him with the same care as if he was in an operating room.

"Finally, Fauville was taken by our troops arriving from Gambosville and La Coquerie. At the same time, coming from the beaches, the first tanks appeared on the main road and we were taken quickly to the front line again, near the village of La Fière, at the edge of the swamp.

"We arrived in the evening, creeping along the embankment through the fields. Shells were hitting the trees, bullets were whistling in the branches or making long furrows in the grass : we were once again in the thick of battle.

"There was a terrible smell coming from the swamps ahead. Swarms of mosquitoes were dancing above the hedges. We could see bright spots of color on the surface of the water, in the reeds and rushes. They were floating parachutes, each with a body, or munitions, or bandages attached. On the other side of the swamp, the Germans were keeping watch.

"We could hear someone moaning in the drinking trough. The chapelain, an American of French origin, had set up a first aid station there. Safe in our holes, all we had to do was wait for our assault troops, who were coming over the hill to continue the fight.

"Our pals told us briefly about their battle. It had certainly been worse than on the road to Carentan. First of all, a lot of the paratroopers had been hurt jumping; many of them had almost drowned.

"The chapelain had decided to say a mass, four hours after the men had landed, to give them courage. He had set up in a little house, and took out his ornements and sacred vessels. Seemingly oblivious to the danger, he prayed for the dead, for those who were suffering, for those who were about to die. The soldiers took turns listening to him.

"They had received a good piece of news. We're not sure, but maybe they heard it on the portable radio. At 4 a.m. on Tuesday, paratroopers guided by French civilians had killed the German general commanding the area and part of his staff, a few kilometers away, at the chateau of Bernaville.

"Then they had run out of munitions gliders and planes had come to resupply them. For 24 hours, they had wondered if they would have to give up the position and retreat to Sainte-Mère-Église. The preceding night, more gliders had landed reinforcements.

"A few hours after we arrived, the chapelain, a round little man, passed by our foxhole. He was in a gay mood; in each hand he was holding a bottle of calvados, which he was taking to the wounded in the drinking trough. He stopped for a moment to tell us he'd found the liquor at a farm. He kept laughing and saying : 'What a story, guys, what a story !'

"Do you know what our friends did during the interruptions between battles? They would search the houses for mementoes. One of them proudly showed us two French decorations from the first world war, which he had asked a veteran for, and which the veteran had given him before leaving the village. Others had a spoon, a fork, or a silver box."

During the first world war, we had done the same sort of thing, under similar circumstances. These men were taking these mementoes home to their ice cold or sunny hot States. Their family and friends were not going to understand why they were so important to them. It's because the past, those days of intense, savage life, of flirting with death, will have cyrstalized on them.

It was time for us to part. It was almost daylight, and our guests had to walk several miles to their camp. Once again, hot coffee was served; tired limbs were begging for sleep.

"Before you leave", I said, "please let me know, quite frankly, what you thought of the civilians you met during your first few days in France."

The blond answered. The other fellow was too busy heating up his little glass of calvados in the palm of his hand, *à la française*.

"We were both wounded a few miles from La Fière by the same shell. We hadn't seen anyone in the village. When we arrived, the inhabitants had been evacuated to Sainte-Mère-Église or to nearby farms, but our pals told us that your countrymen had helped them as much as they could, that on the first night they had showed them where the Germans were, and had given them food and drink, also pointing out the dangerous places in the swamp.

"On the road to Carentan, when the fighting began, we had to threaten some of your countrymen to make them get inside. The shells and bullets were whistling along the ground, and sometimes, from our foxholes, we could see a man or a woman run across the road.

"On Tuesday night, at the height of the battle, an old lady went by. She was going to get help from friends at Fauville, right where the Germans were camped. We were very worried about her, as she walked along in the open among the shells and bullets, along a mined road lined with enemy trenches. As she progressed she got smaller and smaller, and we followed her until she disappeared over the horizon. She never came back."

I told them the rest of the story : as she arrived at Fauville, a German, probably panicking, fired on her from behind a hedge. She agonized for more than two weeks.

"A few days later", continued the paratrooper, "we were near Fresville, on a patrol. A peasant came up to us. He didn't know a word of English and he showed us a paper on which something was written by one of you, in English. It said he was a good Frenchman, well known to all. He managed to tell us that his animals were on the other side, where the Germans were, and that he was going to get them, that he needed milk for the children and wounded. We let him through and he crossed the enemy lines. He walked calmy. The machine guns fell silent on both sides because of him. But the shells continued to burst. He waved to us. He was very brave, but a bit unconscious of the danger !"

The soldiers took their leave, saying once again :
"Good bye. We'll be back some day."

They continued to signal us, by flashing their lights, until they arrived on the main road, at the very same spot where, four months earlier, they had held a war council to decide on the fate of our firemen.

Some day they will come back, I'm sure of it. Their memories will bring them back. Like the first time, C-47s will bring them and their pals. Before landing on the airfield at Cherbourg, they will hedge-hop over Sainte-Mère-Église and, perhaps they will drop flowers picked the day before in the United States, over the cemetaries, like multi-colored parachutes.

June 6th 1945. Little girls in Sainte-Marie-du-Mont honouring US soldiers in front of the monument at Utah Beach.

At Carentan, in front of the town monument, the soldiers celebrate Bastille Day with the children of the town

D-Day anniversary 1952: General Eisenhower shakes hands with one of the « little paratroopers » of Sainte-Mère-Église in front of the first Liberty Milestone erected by the French government shortly after the war.

Decorating the flag and members of the 82nd airborne division (croix de guerre and fourragère) by General Gentilhomme.

A great Franco-American day, June 6th, 1946, at Sainte-Mère-Église.

D Day 1964 commemoration. Mme Simone RENAUD shaking hand with John STEELE.
To her right Bill TUCKER.Behind her Bob MURPHY.

Fort BRAGG N.C. July 1963 . Mr Alexandre RENAUD during an official visit in USA with his son.
In white Colonel Robert PIPER and to his left John STEELE.

35th Anniversary of D DAY. Two visiting 82nd Airborne Veterans: Bob MURPHY (right) a pathfinder dropped one hour before near La Fiére and Karl BECK who was severely wounded upon landing.

XIX

MEMORIES OF SAINTE-MÈRE-ÉGLISE

The months have gone by, and it's the rainy season that comes before the first cold weather. It's been a long time since we last heard the sound of cannon fire.

The victorious army drove across France as fast as its motors could carry it. Mud has now taken the place of dust. Some roads have become impossible and are closed to traffic. Route 13, now called General de Gaulle Street, is nothing but a track that splashes mud up onto the tractor wheels.

Our beaches are still important : they continue to supply the country with war materials. At night, the long convoys go up and down, their headlights on, lighting up the horizon. There are still a few camps. Brilliantly lit up, at night they seem to float on the swamps.

Sainte-Mère-Église's great moment is over.

Two cemetaries seem to keep watch over the town. General Theodore Roosevelt is buried in one, together with his soldiers of the 4th division and the awesome paratroopers. All summer, flowers will grow there, planted by pious hands, thanks to the splendid bravery of these men who clung to our land in supreme sacrifice and prevented our little town from being completely destroyed.

Sainte-Mère-Église, which took the first assault, is nursing its wounds. Notwithstanding the damage, it still has its church and the Roman milestone, which symbolizes our centuries-old history, its big trees, and most of its houses built this way and that over the centuries. It will remain a traditional Normandy town, while others : Valognes, Montebourg, Pont-l'Abbé, will have had to be rebuilt.

It will remain a town of memories, exactly as it appeared to the paratroopers at dawn on June 6th, 1944, just as thousands of Americans who passed through or camped in the surrounding fields saw it, as the shells fell all around and it symbolized to them the heart of liberated France.

Town hall of Sainte-Mère-Église (Manche)
(June-Novembre, 1944)

We would like to thank the following persons, agencies and organizations, which kindly autorized us to reprint the photographs in this book:
- US Army Departement at Washington D.C.
- Photos U.S.I.S.
- Colonel Robert PIPER
- Charles YOUNG
- Weston WAYNES
- Bob LANDRY (Life Magazine)
- M. BENOIT
- Berge AVADENIAN
- Doug STEBELTON (Author of the book and DVD MOTHER OF NORMANDY) - www.motherofnormandy.com
- Yves TARIEL
- Paris-Match Magazine

XX

Annexe

Dear Readers,

I am including a few unpublished documents and pictures which show
the great relationship between the American Airborne Veterans and
Sainte Mère-Eglise.
The Veterans became our friends,our brothers.

Since 1945 we have been eager to express our gratitude and
our deep respect for their sacrifice.

This is our duty of remembrance .

Our friendship for the American people will remain forever.

Maurice RENAUD

June 7th 1945 *- Front page of FRANCE SOIR . The largest French newspaper of that time.*

Drawing by Paul RENAUD *(aged 17 y.o.), the oldest son of Mr and Mme Alexandre RENAUD.*
He was a direct witness of the battle on the church square.
He also designed the famous stained glass window in the church " The VIRGIN MARY and the paratroopers" (see back cover page).

July 1963:
In preparation for the 20th Commemoration of D Day CBS TV organised an interview with General Dwight EISENHOWER and Mme Simone RENAUD.

*Picture taken by Ralph MORSE and published by **LIFE MAGAZINE** in August 1944.*
Mme Simone RENAUD ,the mayor's wife , is laying flowers on General ROOSEVELT 's grave. He was buried in the No 1 cemetery in Sainte-Mère-Eglise.

June 1969 - 25th D Day Anniversary
First massive return of American Veteran paratroopers to Sainte-Mère-Eglise.
Arrival from Paris by special train at the Chef du Pont train station.

JUNE 2004 - RECEPTION GIVEN AT CHATEAU DE L ISLE MARIE TO HONOR THE AMERICAN VETERANS.

Historic picture with: (starting second from left) GENE COOK, RAY FARY, Colonel ROBERT PIPER,
WILLIAM TUCKER, MAURICE RENAUD, ZANE SCHLEMMER, MRS BARBARA GAVIN FAUNTLEROY
(daughter of General GAVIN), BOB MURPHY, BILL SULLIVAN.

March 28th 1982
CHERBOURG MAUPERTUS
YVES TARIEL and BOB MURPHY (to the
right) Picture taken before boarding the
Douglas C 47 now at the Airborne Museum.

TARIEL and MURPHY jumped on the
LA LONDE DZ to celebrate the last flight
of this historic C 47 which,on D Day,
was carrying paratroopers of the 101st A.D.

This plane was part of the 439th Troop Carrier
Group US AIR FORCE.

JUNE 2007 LA FIERE BATTLE MEMORIAL SITE - IRON MIKE -
Pathfinder Airborne Veteran Bob MURPHY with American and British Paratroopers all around him.
The LA FIERE BATTLE MEMORIAL SITE was created by the A V A Association (Friends of the American Veterans).

PICTURE SIGNED BY COLONEL BOB PIPER: *In his foxhole on D Day ,captain Bob PIPER was a member of General Gavin' s staff.He landed at about 500 meters west of Sainte Mere Eglise near the road leading to La Fiere. He did the 4 "Combat Jumps " : SICILY, ITALY, NORMANDY and HOLLAND. A highly experienced soldier he fought also in Korea and Vietnam.*

ARLINGTON NATIONAL CEMETERY
February 8th 2008 : Military Funerals for Colonel Bob PIPER.

ZANE SCHLEMMER (508TH PIR 82nd A.D.) in Sainte Mere Eglise in June 2010.
He landed nearby the chateau de l' Isle Marie on D Day. He was awarded the Legion of Honor
by French President Nicolas SARKOZY at the American cemetery in Colleville sur Mer.
A great friend of Sainte Mere Eglise,ZANE passed away in Florida in 2013.
ZANE was honorary member of the A V A Association and Honorary President of
the "MAUREEN KENNEDY AWARD".

DEPARTMENT OF THE ARMY
HEADQUARTERS 82D AIRBORNE DIVISION
FORT BRAGG, NORTH CAROLINA 28307-5100

March 7, 1988

REPLY TO
ATTENTION OF:

Office of the Commanding General

Monsieur Henri Jean Renaud
50480 Ste Mere Eglise
France

Dear Monsieur Renaud:

All paratroopers of the 82d Airborne Division join
me in expressing our deepest sympathy to you and your
family over the recent death of your mother, Madame Simone
Renaud. We are acutely aware of her great love for freedom, and appreciate her devotion to keeping alive the
memory of the many paratroopers who participated in the
liberation of Ste Mere Eglise and France in June 1944.

She has been a long-time friend of the 82d Airborne
Division, and we will all miss her. Rest assured that even
with the passage of time, we will never forget the troop-
ers who jumped into Ste Mere Eglise and the many kind and
wonderful French citizens who befriended our soldiers,
often taking them into their homes. Many long and rich
friendships came out of that common experience 44 years
ago and still live today. Madame Renaud worked long and
hard for many years to keep alive and cultivate these
mutual friendships. Your loss is most certainly a great
loss to us all.

Please let our many friends in Ste Mere Eglise know
that the paratroopers of the 82d Airborne Division, both
past and present, care very much for them.

With deepest sympathy,

Carl W. Stiner
Major General, U.S. Army
Commanding

*Letters of condoleances sent by General RIDGWAY and Major General Carl W.STINER
commanding the 82nd A.D.in Fort BRAGG N.C. to the RENAUD family after
Mme Simone RENAUD passed away in 1988.*

General M. B. Ridgway
918 W. Waldheim Road Fox Chapel
Pittsburgh, Pennsylvania 15215

20 Feb 88.

Dear M. Renaud,

Mrs. Ridgway and I extend to you, Maurice, Paul
and all other members of the famous Renaud family,
our heartfelt sympathy and respect, in the loss of
your dear Mother.

She is an heroic historic figure, as was and is,
your father, the War time Mayor of Ste Mere Eglise,
and she will always be fondly remembered throughout
the closely knit Airborne fraternity in the United
States Army, as a splendid leader in fostering the
ties between the people of the Ste Mere Eglise region
and our Airborne.

With deep respect I salute the memory of your
parents, as I always shall, the people of Ste Mere
Eglise.

Sincerely,

M. B. Ridgway
General, U.S. Army,
Retired.

FROM: THE MAYOR OF SAINTE MERE EGLISE
TO: MONSIEUR LE COMMISSAIRE DU GOUVERNEMENT DU GENERAL DE GAULLE IN BAYEUX

Monsieur le Commissaire,

On Monday, June 5, at about 11:30 p.m., the thunder of C-47s filled the skies over Normandy. They passed over the treetops, toward the light of a fire that had been set at a house in Sainte Mere Eglise. American paratroopers began jumping into our town.

They were the first of the Allied troops to set their feet on the ground of our enslaved country. Their forces were two battalions: 2nd Battalion and 3rd Battalion of the 505th Parachute Infantry Regiment, 7th U.S. Army, under the command of Lt. Col. Benjamin R. Vandervoort (2nd Battalion) and Lt. Col. Edward C. Krause (3rd Battalion).

Upon their arrival on French soil, they received strong enemy fire from a German flak detachment camped in a park at the center of the town. At dawn, these soldiers, under the command of German Commandant Keller, were driven to the south, to Fauville.

Then, during the next 48 hours, the two U.S. battalions, already diminished by casualties after the night jump, struggled with enemy forces all around them, fighting from isolated positions against the Germans who occupied the eight kilometers between Sainte Mere Eglise and the sea, where the great Allied armada was on its way to the beaches of Normandy. The U.S. battalions inland faced a strong German infantry detachment and the remnants of the flak unit in the village of Fauville. They also fought two German infantry divisions, well-supplied with guns and tanks, in the north, at Neuville Au Plain. To the east, toward Utah Beach, two Georgian companies, fanatic soldiers who vowed to fight to their deaths, were positioned against the Allied forces.

These wonderful American soldiers resisted, on their own, the German and Georgian defenses, with nothing more than their rifles, light machine guns, four heavy machine guns and two small mortars found in gliders.

I observed these American men with great attention. They were quiet and self-controlled, so much so one would think they were on a training maneuver. They smoked cigarettes and chewed gum, holding close to the walls of our town. They advanced against the enemy with firm steps, under continuous shelling from Azeville and the Saint Martin batteries.

In the evening of June 6, from the ditch on the edge of Sainte Mere Eglise, where I had taken refuge with my family and neighbors, I realized that the battle was drawing closer. The two German battalions in Fauville coordinated a counter-attack that was closing in on Sainte Mere Eglise.

During the nights of June 6 and June 7, the battle raged. The Germans had managed to fight their way to the edge of the town. American soldiers were reduced to fighting the enemy with knives. One American paratrooper told me not to worry. "We will counter-attack," he said. "Our forces will arrive from the sea by 6 a.m."

Reinforcements, however, were delayed. "The sea is too rough," one paratrooper told me. Women of our town began to beg and cry. "My God, please don't abandon us," they appealed to the American soldiers.

One paratrooper replied with a comforting smile, "We never abandon anyone. We would rather die here."

Several paratroopers were seen, according to eyewitnesses, riding horseback at full speed to reinforce an American position threatened by enemy forces. Following the battle, we found in the center of town many horses that were killed in the crossfire.

When reinforcements arrived from the sea, we listened with great joy to the sound of U.S. tanks coming in from Ravenoville. The airborne soldiers were nearly out of ammunition by that time. The soldiers told me that they could only shoot when they had a sure kill. "But we still had our bayonets and knives," he said.

Forty-eight hours after landing in Normandy, the airborne soldiers had accomplished an unbelievable mission. On their own, the two American battalions had destroyed two German battalions in the north, one battalion and the flak unit in the south and the two companies of Georgians, whose survivors were forced to take refuge in the Castle of Beuzeville Au Plain. The two American battalions had knocked out eight German tanks and many heavy machine guns. They had taken 364 prisoners.

Casualties were heavy. During that time, a U.S. battalion doctor named Capt. Lyle B. Putnam attended to the French wounded with the same devotion he gave the American soldiers.

Monsieur le Delegue du Gouvernement, I strongly demand that these heroic men, first to free our part of French soil, be honored with glorious citations and the right to wear the French Fourragere.

I think that their sacrifices will appear justified and lighter to them if they are entitled to pin the sign of French gratitude on the flags of their battalions.

In future battles, they will fight even more valiantly, knowing that France has proclaimed these airborne soldiers the bravest of the brave.

With best regards,
Alexandre Renaud
Mayor of Sainte Mere Eglise

cc: Capt. Robert Piper
Adjutant – 505th Parachute Infantry Regiment

The outcome of this letter was that the 82nd Airborne Division was awarded the French CROIX DE GUERRE and the FOURRAGERE by the government of General de Gaulle. (see picture page 153).

THE GREAT CEMETERIES UNDER THE SNOW

Poem written by Mme Simone RENAUD to the American mothers.

THE snow, this night
Has fallen softly from the clouds
To spread its marvelous mantle
On the wooden crosses.

NATURE, for once, has made herself
Merciful and maternel for the poor dead,
By gently weaving thousands of flowers
And thousands of wings (feathers)
In order their shroud might be more soft.

FEATHERS of swans, flowers from heavenly gardens,
A net as light as air
Laid on their last wound and their last gesture,
Like a breath and a kiss...

WHETHER it be the newly born,
Or the pure forehead of the Virgin
Or the silver chalice so bright on the altar,
Nothing is more pure and limpid
Than your flakes falling
From the skies, O snow !

AND who better than you,
Silent and smooth
Could build a more radiant wall
Between the bitter world, sensual and wicked
And these bodies of martyrs given in sacrifice ?

WHAT better than your white shroud
Could separate those who breath only
For vulgar passion, and gold, eating and drinking,
And these proud knights who fell in sacred devotion !

MAY the struggle cease in this holy place.
Also the passion of the living,
For more living are those who died for their dream,
The face toward the rising sun !

KEEP them from ugly things,
Oh beautiful, clear, pure snow.
Push aside all the mud and wickedness
From their sacred ashes.
Be for them a crystal reliquary !

PIOUSLY watch over these shadows in exile,
Rock them, rock them patiently
In your tender arms,
Like a Mother rocks a child !

CONTENTS